The Best Bread Machine Cookbook Ever

The Best Bread Machine Cookbook Ever

Madge Rosenberg

A John Boswell Associates/King Hill Productions Book

HarperCollins*Publishers*

HarperCollins books may be purchased for educational, business, or sales promotional use. For information, please write: Special Markets Department, HarperCollins Publishers, Inc., 10 East 53rd Street, New York, NY 10022.

FIRST EDITION

Design: Barbara Cohen Aronica
Index: Maro Riofrancos

LIBRARY OF CONGRESS CATALOG CARD NUMBER 92-52548
ISBN 0-06-016927-3

92 93 94 95 96 HC 10 9 8 7 6 5 4 3 2 1

Acknowledgments

To Barry,
for his love and encouragement always.
Special thanks to Natalie Andersen
for testing and tasting every recipe.

Contents

Introduction

Welcome to Your Kitchen Bakery

The best bread is freshly baked bread—golden brown, with a warm, heavenly aroma. Since electric bread machines have appeared on the market, there has been a revolution in bread baking: the best bakery in town has moved right into your kitchen.

For *The Best Bread Machine Cookbook Ever,* I adapted all my favorite bread recipes just for the machine and developed any new ones that seemed to be missing. My feeling is that if you have a bakery on your kitchen counter, you should be able to order any kind of bread you want. And the results should be perfect every time. Accordingly, this collection offers an incredible variety of flavors and textures —all guaranteed for success.

The first time I tried an electric bread machine, I couldn't believe how well the bread turned out. It amazed me, in particular, because I am a professional baker. My love affair with bread began with my first part-time job at a bakery as a teenager. Sunday was an especially busy day, as we turned out fragrant loaves of fresh raisin pumpernickel, honey white bread, and German rye for the parishioners returning from church. I found eating that bread made me indescribably happy, and I became happier yet when I learned to make it myself by hand.

This passion for fresh bread was so strong that twenty years, several careers, and three children later, I started my own bakery, Bakery Soutine, on the Upper West Side of Manhattan. Since the shop opened in 1983, we have baked bread for some of the best restaurants and take-out food shops in New York City. And perhaps as a reflection of my taste, I find my customers want interesting breads, bolstered with bran and whole grains, flavored with cheese and vegetables, fragrant with fresh herbs like rosemary and dill.

After so many years of making bread by hand and then with the most sophisticated industrial mixers, dough shapers, and ovens, I was amazed when I tried my first electric bread machine. It was love at first loaf! So little time and energy resulted in such wonderful bread. Even the most finicky doughs, such as buttery brioche and fruit-studded panettone, and the heavy, whole grain blends, tricky for even accomplished bakers to make by hand, came out of the machine perfect every time.

If you have never baked before, nothing could be easier or more gratifying than adding odorless flours and liquids to the machine, walking away, and returning later to unveil fragrant, perfect, just-baked bread. Depending on your mood, you can choose a savory bread, a sweet bread, an exceptionally nutritious bread, or a lovely bread to give to a friend.

In *The Best Bread Machine Cookbook Ever,* you'll find how versatile and easy bread baking is with a machine. I hope these failproof recipes will spur you on to develop your own creativity. Once you become familiar with the order in which ingredients are added to your machine and its particular timing, bread baking can fit right into the busiest working-cook's life.

About the Bread Machines

Bread machines are so popular that new ones are arriving on the market all the time. All the recipes in this book were tested on the models described below. Most notably, no matter what the various cycles offered on the different machines, we found we obtained the best results using the basic bread cycle, or the dough cycle if the bread is removed from the machine for baking.

All of the machines have delayed timing so that you can add the ingredients at your convenience, and the machine will mix and bake the bread up to nine hours later. Fill and set your bread maker at night, and you can wake up to fresh bread. Breads with eggs or other perishables or very heavy matter, such as oats, should not be made on the timed cycle, but sourdoughs work very well.

HITACHI

The Hitachi was the only machine we tried that lets you make a small (7-ounce), medium (14-ounce), or large (1.3-pound) loaf in one machine. We only used the two larger sizes. The water goes in first, then the dry ingredients and yeast. It also makes jam and rice.

PANASONIC OR NATIONAL

The BT65P model of the Panasonic makes a 1½-pound loaf with a really crisp crust and moist interior. There are five cycles on the machine: basic and variety bread cycles, which each take four hours; the whole wheat cycle, which is five hours; crisp bread, seven hours; and a quick bread, which only takes one hour. The dough cycle is two hours and twenty-five minutes, but you can make a large quantity. The basic cycle made such a good crust that the extra three hours on the crisp cycle was not necessary. This is the only machine we used that produced a traditional rectangular loaf shape. There is a separate dispenser for the yeast. It is released fifteen minutes into the cycle at the end of the first kneading. This is also the time to add raisins, nuts, etc. since there is no beeper to indicate the time to add them.

REGAL
The removable crumb tray in the Regal makes it one of the easiest machines to keep clean. It also has indicators that let you know just what stage you are at in the process: kneading, rising, baking. There is a raisin bread cycle with a beeper and a bread cycle, each taking three hours plus a cool down. The dough cycle is one hour and twenty-five minutes. In this machine, start with the liquids, then add the dry ingredients, and lastly the yeast.

SANYO
The Sanyo has a three-hour bread cycle with a buzzer to let you know when to add raisins, nuts, and the like, and a one hour and fifteen-minute dough cycle. The variety breads are excellent in this machine, even without a separate cycle, because the Sanyo distributes add-ins very well. Here the dry ingredients are added first, then the flour, and the yeast last.

WELBILT
The smaller Welbilt is the fastest machine. It bakes a one-pound loaf in two hours and fifteen minutes, makes dough in fifty minutes, and does a good job of it. There is a buzzer for adding ingredients. The yeast goes in first, then the dry ingredients, followed by the liquids. The larger size has a domed glass top and a four-hour bread cycle.

ZOJIRUSHI

We used the large machine that produces an almost eight-inch-high loaf in four hours. There is a glass insert in the top for viewing. The six cycles are basic, quick, raisin, French bread, dough, and cake and jam, plus a "Homemade Menu" to program yourself. This machine requires that you start with the liquids, then add the dry ingredients and lastly the yeast.

DAK

This machine is available through the DAK catalog, which has an 800 telephone number. It is reputed to be similar to the Welbilt, but we did not discover it until too late in our research to test it.

About the Ingredients

ACTIVE DRY YEAST

Yeast is made of tiny plants that change food—especially gluten and sugar—into carbon dioxide, which causes the bread to rise. Keep active dry yeast in the refrigerator. The machines are not timed for instant yeast or for fresh cake yeast, so use only *active dry yeast.*

BARLEY MALT SYRUP

This is extracted by sprouting and drying barley, which is a grain, and caramelizing its sugar. It adds a rich, barely sweet taste, while encouraging the yeast and sourdough to rise and produce richer, moister bread. It is available in health food stores.

CARAMEL COLORING

Some people think that the blacker the bread, the healthier; but most really dark breads are colored with burned sugar or caramel syrup. It sweetens the bread only slightly, but adds moisture as well as color. Making your own will ruin a pot and possibly your kitchen. A good mail-order source is listed on page 11.

EGGS

Eggs add flavor and lightness and a golden color to bread. Egg substitutes can be used in any of these breads.

FATS

Oils, butter, margarine, lard, chicken fat, and solid vegetable shortening are all fats that make bread softer and tastier and preserve it longer. When oil is called for, unless olive oil is specified, use a flavorless polyunsaturated vegetable oil, such as safflower, canola, corn, or a mixed vegetable oil.

SALT

Salt not only adds flavor, it governs the power of the yeast. Salt slows down the yeast action; too much salt can kill the yeast. Too little salt lets the dough rise so fast that it may fall before it finishes baking. Salt is also a preservative, which keeps the bread from getting stale as quickly. Without salt, bread has a coarser quality because of the overly fast rising.

SOURDOUGH STARTER

This is an ingredient to keep on hand so you can make sourdough bread anytime: Mix 1 cup of flour with 1 cup of water and a pinch of yeast. Stir until creamy. Leave the mixture alone for a week in a large glass or plastic container, unrefrigerated. It is a living culture that bubbles and smells weird. The different strains of yeast in the atmosphere work on it. Sours made from the same ingredients vary from place to place because of the ambient conditions. No one has made San Francisco sourdough in the Midwest yet, although commercial bakeries have tried.

At least once a week, use your starter or discard ½ cup of it, and be sure to replenish it with equal amounts of flour and water stirred together until they are smooth and creamy. This keeps the starter fresh and active. After the initial week, you can store the starter in the refrigerator, but bring it up to room temperature for baking by making the water in the recipe just warmer than body temperature and mixing the two together before they go into the bread machine.

SWEETENERS

Sugar, brown sugar, honey, molasses, and fruits add sweetness and help brown the crust. The riper the fruit, the more sweetness it adds. Dried fruit adds concentrated sweetness.

WHEAT

Bread flour is high-gluten, or hard, wheat without its germ or bran but containing all the gluten from the grain. It rises better than any other flour because the gluten forms the walls around the carbon dioxide bubbles from the action of the yeast.

Whole wheat flour has the bran and the germ but a lower proportion of gluten. It rises, but not as well as bread flour. Buy whole wheat bread flour, not pastry flour, and choose the coarsest grind you can find; it is sometimes called graham flour.

Wheat bran is the outside of the wheat kernel. It contains much of the vitamins and most of the fiber.

Wheat germ is the center of the wheat kernel and it contains many nutrients and oils. Once a jar of wheat germ is opened, it should be refrigerated. Because of the high concentration of oil, it can go rancid quickly at room temperature.

Semolina is a wheat usually used for pasta. Made from durum wheat, it is strong and rises well.

Wheatberry is the whole, unground kernel of wheat. It is highly nutritious. Because it is so hard, it must be cooked for about an hour or soaked overnight before it is used in baking. Wheatberries contribute a nutty taste and a wonderful bite to bread. Softened or sprouted wheatberries can be added to salads.

Cracked wheat is the whole wheat kernel crushed into very small pieces but still coarser than the coarsest whole wheat flour. Some people soak it for an hour before using; I prefer not to because I like the crunch.

Bulgur is parboiled, dried, and cracked wheat kernels.

OTHER FLOURS AND GRAINS

Amaranth is a nutty, high-protein grain from Central America. Since it is very low in gluten, use small quantities along with a large amount of wheat flour. It has a bland flavor.

Barley is an ancient grain with a distinctive, almost flat flavor; it has very little gluten. Rather than barley flour, use barley flakes, which add texture as well as taste.

Cornmeal adds its own slightly sweet flavor, crumbly texture, and sunny color to bread if you use yellow cornmeal, as we did. Stone-ground meal is most distinctive, but the supermarket variety will serve.

Oats are just regular, old-fashioned oatmeal or, specifically, rolled oats. The same oats you use for breakfast cereal add their flavor and fiber to bread. All the oat bran is still there. Toast oats lightly in a 350 degree oven for 5 minutes to intensify their flavor.

Quinoa is a nutritious pearly grain from Peru, recently brought into the United States and popularized because of its high protein and mineral content.

Rye flour is high in protein, but low in gluten. Consequently, it will not rise on its own. From 20 to 30 percent of the flour content in a bread can be rye; but the rest needs to be high-gluten wheat flour, or you will have very heavy bread. White rye flour is used in "rye bread"; dark rye is used for "pumpernickel."

Soy flour is extremely high in protein and adds moisture to bread. Since it is so low in gluten and in texture, do not make it more than one quarter the flour content.

Triticale flour is a hybrid of wheat and rye, nicely flavored but in need of gluten. It has to be used with double its measure of bread flour.

Sources of Supplies

BARLEY MALT SYRUP AND CARAMEL COLORING

Niblack Foods, Inc.
900 Jefferson Road, Blding. # 5
Rochester, NY 14623
(716) 292-0790

CARAMEL COLORING

Mister Spiceman
169–06 Crocheron Avenue
Auburndale, NY 11358
(718) 358-5020

FLOURS AND GRAINS

Arrowhead Mills
110 So. Lawton
Hereford, TX 79045
(806) 364-0730

Deer Valley Farm
Box 173
Guilford, NY 13780-0173
(607) 764-8556

Elams
2625 Gardner Road
Broadview, IL 60153
(708) 865-1612

King Arthur Flour
RR 2 Box 56
Norwich, VT 05055
(800) 827-6836

Walnut Acres
Penns Creek, PA 17862
(800) 433-3998

Measuring

Read your owner's manual, because bread machines differ. Ingredients are put in in different orders, temperature requirements for the liquids differ, and minimum and maximum amounts of bread flour differ. In using any recipe in this book, be sure to follow the manufacturer's instructions. For best results, measure ingredients precisely. Too much liquid results in soggy, sunken breads. Too much flour makes bread heavy, coarse, and dry.

DRY INGREDIENTS
Measure over a plate or paper towel. Spoon flours, granulated sugar, and grains into a measuring cup until overflowing. Do not press down. Level by sweeping the excess off with an unserrated knife or spatula.

BROWN SUGAR AND BUTTER OR MARGARINE
Press firmly into a dry measuring cup or spoon. Level off the excess with an unserrated knife or spatula. If using brown sugar, sprinkle it into the flour; do not add in a single lump.

LIQUIDS
Use a standard liquid measuring cup and spoons. Check measurement at eye level.

STICKY INGREDIENTS (HONEY, MOLASSES, AND SO ON)
Oil cup or spoon first so that the sticky stuff will slide out easily. If the recipe calls for butter or oil, measure it first and the sticky ingredient second so you won't have to wash the measure in between.

Freezing

To freeze baked bread, let the loaf cool completely. Wrap the whole unsliced bread in plastic wrap, foil, or freezer paper, forcing out as much air as possible. To defrost, leave the bread wrapped at room temperature for two hours or overnight. Unwrap for another hour so that it will not be soggy. For quicker thawing, slice the bread before freezing.

To warm defrosted bread, place it in a preheated 300 degree oven for 15 to 20 minutes.

It is better to bake bread before freezing it. But if you want to freeze unbaked dough that has completed the dough cycle in the bread machine, brush it lightly with oil, wrap it well, and freeze. Keep the dough frozen for no more than two days, or it will lose its ability to rise. Richer doughs containing butter and sugar freeze best. To defrost, unwrap, cover loosely, and defrost overnight in the refrigerator. When defrosted, leave at room temperature in a draft-free place to rise. Do not leave dough unrefrigerated while defrosting, or the outside will begin to rise before the inside defrosts.

Helpful Hints

1. Before you slice or juice an orange or a lemon, peel off the zest, the colored part of the skin, with a swivel-bladed vegetable peeler. Save it for the many recipes that call for orange and lemon zest, candied or plain.

2. Before using nuts and seeds, toast them lightly in a 350 degree oven for about 5 minutes to bring out the flavor and cool.

3. Keep a piece of bread in an opened box of brown sugar. The sugar will stay soft; the bread will get hard.

4. When you remove baked bread from the machine, keep the loaf inverted until it is just cool enough to handle; then check to be sure the kneading blade has not remained in the loaf. If it has, remove it before turning the bread right side up. If you slice the bread with the blade still in it you will scrape the blade and remove some of the nonstick coating.

5. If your machine has a clear domed top and your bread is not browning, cover the top of the machine with aluminum foil to help the bread brown.

6. To store bread, place it in a plastic bag with a rib of celery to keep it fresher. Seal and store in a cool dry place. I find bread gets soggy in the refrigerator.

Common Problems and Their Solutions

PROBLEM	CAUSE	SOLUTION
1. Sunken top	Bread falls because dough is too wet	Reduce liquid by 1 tablespoon or add 2 tablespoons of flour.
2. Knotty, uneven top	Not enough moisture	Add 1 tablespoon of liquid or reduce flour by 2 tablespoons.
3. Mushroom top	Bread rises too fast and collapses	Reduce yeast by ¼ teaspoon.
4. Slices unevenly	Bread is too hot	Let bread cool before slicing.
5. Top is raw	Too much dough	Reduce size of recipe by 10 to 20 percent.
6. Pocket of sticky dough in sweet breads	Too much sugar or too little yeast	Add ¼ teaspoon yeast or reduce the sugar by 1 tablespoon.

Chapter One

Deli and Basic Sandwich Breads

You can always judge a delicatessen by its bread. No matter how good the corned beef or smoked turkey, you cannot have a great sandwich without fresh, moist bread.

If you want sandwiches filled with sliced meat, maybe coleslaw and mustard or mayonnaise, use any of the breads in this chapter. They are hearty enough to hold up to the spiciest cold cuts, but are not too overpowering to eat toasted with scrambled eggs at breakfast. They have personalities of their own, but need not hold center stage. While they have great texture, let the sandwich fillings star. Most deli breads are best completely cooled and sliced ½ inch thick, especially if you are going to fill them. Don't be stingy.

None of these breads is hard to make. Even though these breads taste as if they were made by professionals, in the bread machine they take only ten minutes of even a novice baker's time. Just fill the bread machine and press the button. After a few soft yet crusty loaves, you will be totally at ease with your bread machine and in the habit of having the earthy smell and taste of fresh bread at any time. Baking bread in your machine will become as easy and habitual as brewing coffee or tea.

Honey White Bread

If you want familiar, comforting, soft bread, the favorite of children everywhere, try this one. Honey White Bread is perfect for breakfast toast with fried eggs, it makes fine tuna or peanut butter and jelly sandwiches, and it's great for BLT's.

SMALL LOAF (1 POUND)	INGREDIENTS	LARGE LOAF (1½ POUNDS)
¾ cup plus 2 tablespoons	milk	1¼ cups
2 tablespoons	unsalted butter	3 tablespoons
1½ tablespoons	honey	2 tablespoons
1 teaspoon	active dry yeast	1½ teaspoons
2 cups	bread flour	3 cups
½ teaspoon	salt	¾ teaspoon

1. Scald the milk. Remove from the heat and add in the butter and honey. Stir until the butter melts. Let cool to room temperature.

2. Add the milk mixture and all remaining ingredients in the order suggested by your bread machine manual and process on the basic bread cycle according to the manufacturer's directions. The bread is good warm, cool, or toasted. It stales faster than store-bought white bread, so wrap the loaf well and use quickly or freeze.

Basic Lean White Bread

This airy, crusty, fat-free loaf is perfect sandwich bread for tunafish, peanut butter, or lettuce and tomato. If you don't slice it too thick, it will even fit into a low-calorie diet. Since this recipe has no shortening, the bread will turn stale after only one day, but it will still make fine toast, especially good for a fried egg sandwich.

SMALL LOAF (1 POUND)	INGREDIENTS	LARGE LOAF (1½ POUNDS)
1 teaspoon	active dry yeast	1½ teaspoons
2 cups	bread flour	3 cups
1 teaspoon	salt	1½ teaspoons
1 tablespoon	sugar	1½ tablespoons
¾ cup plus 1 tablespoon	water	1¼ cups

Add all ingredients in the order suggested by your bread machine manual and process on the basic bread cycle according to the manufacturer's directions. Let the loaf cool for 15 minutes before slicing.

American Garlic and Parsley Bread

This is good bread for a steak sandwich, French dip roast beef, or a grilled mozzarella cheese and tomato sandwich. Baking the garlic right in the bread lightens the garlic flavor. If this is not a strong enough garlic statement for you, add another clove.

SMALL LOAF (1 POUND)	INGREDIENTS	LARGE LOAF (1½ POUNDS)
1 teaspoon	active dry yeast	1½ teaspoons
2 cups	bread flour	3 cups
2 tablespoons	wheat germ	3 tablespoons
2 tablespoons	wheat bran	3 tablespoons
1¼ teaspoons	salt	1¾ teaspoons
1 tablespoon	sugar	1½ tablespoons
1 tablespoon	vegetable oil	1½ tablespoons
1	garlic clove, minced	2
2 tablespoons	chopped fresh parsley	3 tablespoons
¾ cup plus 1 teaspoon	water	1¼ cups

Add all ingredients in the order suggested by your bread machine manual and process on the basic bread cycle according to the manufacturer's directions. Let the loaf cool before slicing. Serve plain or toasted.

Brownie Bread

This bread is for kids of all ages. It is heavenly warm with cold milk or spread with peanut butter that is then softened by the warmth of the bread. Make sweet sandwiches with raspberry jam. Cut them small for tea or lunch boxes.

SMALL LOAF (1 POUND)	INGREDIENTS	LARGE LOAF (1½ POUNDS)
¾ cup	water	1 cup plus 2 tablespoons
⅓ cup	unsweetened cocoa powder	½ cup
1½ teaspoons	active dry yeast	2½ teaspoons
1¾ cups plus 2 tablespoons	bread flour	3 cups
½ cup	sugar	¾ cup
1 teaspoon	salt	1½ teaspoons
1½ tablespoons	vegetable oil	2 tablespoons
1	whole egg	1
0	egg yolk	1
⅓ cup	walnut pieces	½ cup

1. Bring the water to a boil. Add the cocoa and stir until completely dissolved. Let cool to room temperature.

2. Add the cocoa and all remaining ingredients except the nuts in the order suggested by your bread machine manual and process on the basic bread cycle according to the manufacturer's directions.

3. At the beeper (or at the end of the first kneading in the Panasonic or National), add the walnuts.

Corn and Cheddar Bread

Slices of Corn and Cheddar Bread filled with turkey, avocado, tomato, and mayonnaise make a wonderful sandwich, especially if you can eat it under an umbrella next to a pool. Serve with gazpacho or nibble this bread with chili or huevos rancheros.

SMALL LOAF (1 POUND)	INGREDIENTS	LARGE LOAF (1½ POUNDS)
¾ cup plus 2 tablespoons	milk	1¼ cups
1½ tablespoons	honey	2 tablespoons
2 tablespoons	butter	3 tablespoons
1½ teaspoons	active dry yeast	2½ teaspoons
1⅔ cups	bread flour	2½ cups
⅔ cup	yellow cornmeal	1 cup
1 teaspoon	salt	1½ teaspoons
½ cup	grated Cheddar cheese	⅔ cup

1. Scald the milk. Stir in the honey and butter and let cool to room temperature.
2. Add the milk mixture and all remaining ingredients except the Cheddar cheese in the order suggested by your bread machine manual and process on the basic bread cycle according to the manufacturer's directions.
3. At the beeper (or at the end of the first kneading in the Panasonic or National), add the cheese.

Tex-Mex Cornbread

This is spicy enough to call for beer or cold lemonade. Fill slices with Monterey jack cheese or mild Cheddar for a Texas toasted cheese sandwich.

SMALL LOAF (1 POUND)	INGREDIENTS	LARGE LOAF (1½ POUNDS)
1¼ teaspoons	active dry yeast	2 teaspoons
1½ cups	bread flour	2¼ cups
¾ cup	yellow cornmeal	1 cup plus 2 tablespoons
2 tablespoons	wheat germ	3 tablespoons
2 teaspoons	ground cumin	1 tablespoon
2 teaspoons	chili powder	1 tablespoon
2 tablespoons	minced cilantro	3 tablespoons
1¼ teaspoons	salt	2 teaspoons
1 tablespoon	sugar	1½ tablespoons
2 tablespoons	vegetable oil	3 tablespoons
1	whole egg	1
0	egg yolk	1
⅔ cup	water	1 cup
1 teaspoon	minced jalapeño pepper	1½ teaspoons
½ cup	corn kernels	¾ cup

1. Add all ingredients except the jalapeño pepper and corn in the order suggested by your bread machine manual and process on the basic bread cycle according to the manufacturer's directions.

2. At the beeper (or at the end of the first kneading in the Panasonic or National), add the pepper and corn.

Soutine's Rosemary Whole Wheat

You can buy our signature loaf at Fairway or Zabar's in New York City—we make it for them—or you can make it yourself. Slice, spread with a mix of mustard and mayonnaise, and fill with chicken salad or smoked turkey. Lamb or beef stew taste good with it, too.

SMALL LOAF (1 POUND)	INGREDIENTS	LARGE LOAF (1½ POUNDS)
1½ teaspoons	active dry yeast	2½ teaspoons
½ cup	bread flour	¾ cup
1¾ cups	whole wheat flour	2⅔ cups
2 tablespoons	wheat bran	3 tablespoons
2 teaspoons	dried rosemary	1 tablespoon
1 teaspoon	salt	1½ teaspoons
3 tablespoons	vegetable oil	¼ cup
3 tablespoons	honey	¼ cup
¾ cup	water	1 cup plus 2 tablespoons

Add all ingredients in the order suggested by your bread machine manual and process on the basic bread cycle according to the manufacturer's directions.

Country Bread

You can take this bread anywhere with anything. Slice it thick and toast for bacon and eggs; slice thin and toast for caviar. Grill with Cheddar and tomato or with Swiss cheese and ham. Fill with Russian dressing, sliced radishes, cucumbers, and sprouts for a vegetarian lunch.

SMALL LOAF (1 POUND)	INGREDIENTS	LARGE LOAF (1½ POUNDS)
1¼ teaspoons	active dry yeast	2 teaspoons
1⅓ cups	bread flour	2 cups
⅔ cup	whole wheat flour	1 cup
2 tablespoons	wheat germ	3 tablespoons
1 tablespoon	sugar	1½ tablespoons
1 teaspoon	salt	1½ teaspoons
1 tablespoon	vegetable oil	1½ tablespoons
½ cup	sourdough starter (page 7) *	¾ cup
⅔ cup	water	1 cup

Add all the ingredients in the order suggested by your bread machine manual and process on the basic bread cycle according to the manufacturer's directions.

* After measuring out what is needed for this recipe, be sure to replenish your sourdough starter with equal amounts of flour and water.

Dilled Potato Bread

Leftover or just cooked and mashed potatoes give this bread a soft texture and tangy, almost sourdough taste. The loaf is very good with pot roast or roast beef, meat loaf, vegetable soups, and chowders.

SMALL LOAF (1 POUND)	INGREDIENTS	LARGE LOAF (1½ POUNDS)
1 teaspoon	active dry yeast	1½ teaspoons
2 cups	bread flour	3 cups
2 tablespoons	wheat germ	3 tablespoons
2 tablespoons	powdered milk	3 tablespoons
1 tablespoon	sugar	1½ tablespoons
1 teaspoon	dill seed	1½ teaspoons
1¼ teaspoons	salt	2 teaspoons
1 tablespoon	vegetable oil	1½ tablespoons
½ cup	mashed potato	¾ cup
1	whole egg	1
0	egg yolk	1
¾ cup	water	1 cup plus 2 tablespoons

Add all ingredients in the order suggested by your bread machine manual and process on the basic bread cycle according to the manufacturer's directions. When warm, cut into thick slices. For slices less than ½ inch thick, let cool before cutting.

American Pumpernickel

Here is an easy-to-eat dark bread that goes well with everything from scrambled eggs for breakfast to smoked salmon for canapés after the opera to peanut butter sandwiches for school lunch.

SMALL LOAF (1 POUND)	INGREDIENTS	LARGE LOAF (1½ POUNDS)
1½ teaspoons	active dry yeast	2½ teaspoons
1½ cups	bread flour	2¼ cups
⅔ cup	rye flour	1 cup
3 tablespoons	cornmeal	¼ cup
2 tablespoons	powdered milk	3 tablespoons
1 tablespoon	vegetable oil	1½ tablespoons
1½ tablespoons	honey	2 tablespoons
1 teaspoon	caraway seeds	1½ teaspoons
1 teaspoon	salt	1½ teaspoons
1 teaspoon	caramel coloring*	1½ teaspoons
¾ cup plus 2 tablespoons	water	1¼ cups

Add all ingredients in the order suggested by your bread machine manual and process on the basic bread cycle according to the manufacturer's directions.

* Mail-order source on page 11.

Buttermilk Pumpernickel

This nutritious black bread is perfect with hearty soups, with soft mild cheeses from ricotta to brie, and with smoked ham or turkey. Plain low-fat yogurt can be substituted for the buttermilk.

SMALL LOAF (1 POUND)	INGREDIENTS	LARGE LOAF (1½ POUNDS)
1¼ teaspoons	active dry yeast	1¾ teaspoons
1½ cups	bread flour	2¼ cups
¾ cup	rye flour	1 cup plus 2 tablespoons
1 tablespoon	brown sugar	1½ tablespoons
1 teaspoon	salt	1½ teaspoons
1 tablespoon	vegetable oil	1½ tablespoons
1 tablespoon	caramel coloring*	1½ tablespoons
¼ cup	buttermilk	⅓ cup
¾ cup	water	1 cup plus 2 tablespoons

Add all ingredients in the order suggested by your bread machine manual and process on the basic bread cycle according to the manufacturer's directions.

* Mail-order source on page 11.

New York Raisin Pumpernickel

New York's fanciest restaurants, best bakeries, and toniest delicatessens boast this sort of dense black bread chock-full of raisins.

SMALL LOAF (1 POUND)	INGREDIENTS	LARGE LOAF (1½ POUNDS)
1¼ teaspoons	active dry yeast	2½ teaspoons
1¼ cups	bread flour	1¾ cups plus 2 tablespoons
⅔ cup	rye flour	1 cup
1½ teaspoons	caraway seeds	1 tablespoon
1 teaspoon	salt	1½ teaspoons
1 tablespoon	vegetable oil	1½ tablespoons
1 tablespoon	caramel coloring*	1½ tablespoons
½ cup	sourdough starter (page 7)**	⅔ cup
⅔ cup	water	1 cup
1 cup	raisins	1½ cups

1. Add all ingredients except the raisins in the order suggested by your bread machine manual and process on the basic bread cycle according to the manufacturer's directions.

2. At the beeper (or at the end of the first kneading in the Panasonic or National), add the raisins. Let the loaf cool before slicing.

* Mail-order source on page 11.

** After measuring out what is needed for this recipe, be sure to replenish your sourdough starter with equal amounts of flour and water.

Russian Pumpernickel

Dark in color but light in texture, this is an excellent moist sandwich bread for roast beef, pot roast, turkey, or tuna, or to serve with borscht or vegetable or chicken soup.

SMALL LOAF (1 POUND)	INGREDIENTS	LARGE LOAF (1½ POUNDS)
1½ teaspoons	active dry yeast	2½ teaspoons
1½ cups plus 2 tablespoons	bread flour	2½ cups
¾ cup	rye flour	1 cup plus 2 tablespoons
½ cup	grated raw boiling potato, skin on	¾ cup
1 teaspoon	salt	1½ teaspoons
1 tablespoon	sugar	1½ tablespoons
1 tablespoon	dill seed	1½ tablespoons
2 teaspoons	caramel coloring*	1 tablespoon
2 tablespoons	vinegar	3 tablespoons
1 tablespoon	vegetable oil	1½ tablespoons
½ cup	water	¾ cup

Add all ingredients in the order suggested by your bread machine manual and process on the basic bread cycle according to the manufacturer's directions.

* Mail-order source on page 11.

Sourdough Pumpernickel

The liveliest yet lightest textured dark bread makes excellent ham and cheese sandwiches and cries out for mustard. Gruyère, blue cheese, or sharp Cheddar cheese taste best on this loaf, which stands up to but does not conflict with these assertive cheeses.

SMALL LOAF (1 POUND)	INGREDIENTS	LARGE LOAF (1½ POUNDS)
1 teaspoon	active dry yeast	1½ teaspoons
1¼ cups	bread flour	2 cups
½ cup	wheat bran	¾ cup
⅔ cup	rye flour	1 cup
1 teaspoon	caraway seeds	1½ teaspoons
2 tablespoons	brown sugar	3 tablespoons
1½ teaspoons	caramel coloring*	2 teaspoons
1 tablespoon	unsweetened cocoa powder	1½ tablespoons
1 teaspoon	salt	1½ teaspoons
1 tablespoon	vegetable oil	1½ tablespoons
½ cup	sourdough starter (page 7)**	¾ cup
⅔ cup	water	¾ cup

Add all ingredients in the order suggested by your bread machine manual and process on the basic bread cycle according to the manufacturer's directions.

* Mail-order source on page 11.

** After measuring out what is needed for this recipe, be sure to replenish your sourdough starter with equal amounts of flour and water.

Whole Wheat Pumpernickel

Because this fine-grained bread slices so well, it is excellent for thin, Danish open-faced sandwiches topped with smoked or pickled fish, shrimp, or sliced smoked ham or turkey. Or pile on crisp vegetables with a mustard and mayonnaise dressing.

SMALL LOAF (1 POUND)	INGREDIENTS	LARGE LOAF (1½ POUNDS)
¾ cup plus 2 tablespoons	milk	1⅓ cups
1½ teaspoons	active dry yeast	2¼ teaspoons
1¾ cups	whole wheat flour	2⅔ cups
¾ cup	rye flour	1 cup plus 2 tablespoons
1 tablespoon	caraway seeds	1½ tablespoons
2 teaspoons	grated orange zest	1 tablespoon
1 teaspoon	salt	1½ teaspoons
1 tablespoon	caramel coloring*	1½ tablespoons
1	whole egg	1
0	egg yolk	1
1 tablespoon	butter	1½ tablespoons
1 tablespoon	brown sugar	1½ tablespoons

1. Scald the milk. Let cool to room temperature.

2. Add all ingredients in the order suggested by your bread machine manual and process on the basic bread cycle according to the manufacturer's directions. Let the loaf cool completely. Slice thinly.

* Mail-order source on page 11.

Sourdough Lean and Simple

An unpretentious bread that is full of character, this fat-free sourdough is good for Italian salami or prosciutto sandwiches or as an accompaniment to fish or clam chowder, or to pasta. Toast thick slices of the bread and rub with garlic and brush with olive oil to make real Italian garlic bread—bruschetta.

SMALL LOAF (1 POUND)	INGREDIENTS	LARGE LOAF (1½ POUNDS)
1 teaspoon	active dry yeast	1½ teaspoons
1¾ cups	bread flour	2⅔ cups
1 tablespoon	sugar	1½ tablespoons
1 teaspoon	salt	1½ teaspoons
⅔ cup	sourdough starter* (page 7)	1 cup
½ cup	water	¾ cup

Add all ingredients in the order suggested by your bread machine manual and process on the basic bread cycle according to the manufacturer's directions. Let the loaf cool before slicing.

* Be sure to replenish the sourdough starter by adding ½ cup of water and ½ cup of flour to the remaining starter. Stir until combined and creamy.

Sourdough Whole Wheat Bread
with Cheddar Cheese

This rugged bread keeps for days, travels well, and makes great bacon, lettuce, and tomato sandwiches. Serve with cream of tomato soup or Manhattan clam chowder, burgers, or chili. Toast for fried egg sandwiches.

SMALL LOAF (1 POUND)	INGREDIENTS	LARGE LOAF (1½ POUNDS)
1½ teaspoons	active dry yeast	2 teaspoons
1⅓ cups	bread flour	2 cups
⅔ cup	whole wheat flour	1 cup
⅓ cup	wheat bran	½ cup
1 teaspoon	salt	1½ teaspoons
1 tablespoon plus 1 teaspoon	brown sugar	2 tablespoons
1 tablespoon	vegetable oil	1½ tablespoons
1 cup	sourdough starter (page 7) *	1½ cups
⅓ cup	water	½ cup
½ cup	grated Cheddar cheese	¾ cup

1. Add all ingredients except Cheddar cheese in the order suggested by your bread machine manual and process on the basic bread cycle according to the manufacturer's directions.

2. At the beeper (or at the end of the first kneading in the Panasonic or National), add the cheese.

* After measuring out what is needed for this recipe, be sure to replenish your sourdough starter with equal amounts of flour and water.

Light Whole Wheat Bread

Light in texture, color, taste, and calories when sliced thin, this bread makes good tuna, chicken, egg salad, cold meat, or peanut butter sandwiches. For a tacowich: Toast bread slices, top with leftover chili, grated Cheddar or jack cheese, and broil until cheese melts. Stop there and eat, or add shredded lettuce, pickled jalapeños, and chopped tomatoes or salsa on top.

SMALL LOAF (1 POUND)	INGREDIENTS	LARGE LOAF (1½ POUNDS)
1½ teaspoons	active dry yeast	2¼ teaspoons
1 cup plus 2 tablespoons	bread flour	1⅔ cups
1 cup	whole wheat flour	1½ cups
1 teaspoon	salt	1½ teaspoons
1 tablespoon	vegetable oil	1½ tablespoons
2 tablespoons	honey	3 tablespoons
¾ cup plus 1 tablespoon	water	1¼ cups

Add all ingredients in the order suggested by your bread machine manual and process on the basic bread cycle according to the manufacturer's directions.

Whole Wheat Coffee Cake

Fragrant with cinnamon and slightly sweet, this cakey bread is perfect for breakfast. If you are trying to learn to like whole wheat bread, here is a recipe that can help you make the transition toward whole grains.

SMALL LOAF (1 POUND)	INGREDIENTS	LARGE LOAF (1½ POUNDS)
⅔ cup	milk	1 cup
2 tablespoons	butter	3 tablespoons
2 tablespoons	honey	3 tablespoons
1½ teaspoons	active dry yeast	2¼ teaspoons
¾ cup	bread flour	1⅓ cups
¾ cup	whole wheat flour	1 cup plus 2 tablespoons
2 tablespoons	wheat bran	3 tablespoons
½ teaspoon	salt	¾ teaspoon
1	whole egg(s)	2
1	egg yolk	1
3 tablespoons	brown sugar	¼ cup
1 teaspoon	ground cinnamon	1½ teaspoons
⅓ cup	raisins	½ cup

1. Scald the milk. Stir in the butter and honey and let cool to room temperature.

2. Add the milk mixture and all remaining ingredients except the brown sugar, ½ teaspoon of the cinnamon, and the raisins in the order suggested by your bread machine manual and process on the basic bread cycle according to the manufacturer's directions.

3. At the beeper (or at the end of the first kneading in the Panasonic or National), add the remainder of the cinnamon, brown sugar, and raisins.

Apple Onion Rye

This barely sweet, fruity rye tastes good with scrambled eggs or in a turkey sandwich. For tea sandwiches, slice thin and spread with cream cheese and toasted sliced almonds.

SMALL LOAF (1 POUND)	INGREDIENTS	LARGE LOAF (1½ POUNDS)
1½ teaspoons	active dry yeast	2¼ teaspoons
1¼ cups	bread flour	1¾ cups plus 2 tablespoons
1 cup	rye flour	1½ cups
¼ cup	cracked wheat	⅓ cup
1 tablespoon	sugar	1½ tablespoons
1 teaspoon	salt	1½ teaspoons
1 teaspoon	caraway seeds	1½ teaspoons
1	garlic clove(s), minced	2
1 small	onion, minced	1 medium
1 medium	apple, chopped	1 large
2 tablespoons	unsalted butter	3 tablespoons
⅓ cup	water	½ cup

Add all ingredients in the order suggested by your bread machine manual and process on the basic bread cycle according to the manufacturer's directions. Let the loaf cool completely before slicing.

Delicatessen Rye

Here is the classic tangy, chewy rye sandwich bread that you find at first-rate delicatessens. Fill slices with cold cuts, strong-flavored cheeses, such as havarti or Gruyère, or with tuna salad. This is the bread for a classic Reuben sandwich.

SMALL LOAF (1 POUND)	INGREDIENTS	LARGE LOAF (1½ POUNDS)
1½ teaspoons	active dry yeast	2¼ teaspoons
1¾ cups	bread flour	2⅔ cups
¾ cup	rye flour	1 cup plus 2 tablespoons
1½ teaspoons	sugar	2¼ teaspoons
1 teaspoon	salt	1½ teaspoons
1 tablespoon	caraway seeds	1½ tablespoons
1 tablespoon	vegetable oil	1½ tablespoons
1 teaspoon	barley malt syrup *	1½ teaspoons
¼ cup	sourdough starter (page 7) **	⅓ cup
¾ cup	water	1 cup plus 2 tablespoons

Add all ingredients in the order suggested by your bread machine manual and process on the basic bread cycle according to the manufacturer's directions.

* Available in health food stores.

** After measuring out what is needed for this recipe, be sure to replenish your sourdough starter with equal amounts of flour and water.

Malted Rye Bread

Since the flavor of this loaf is not too assertive, but the texture is substantial, it is a good sandwich bread for spicy meats, such as salami or pâté, and ripe cheese. For early-in-the-day eating, toast and spread with orange marmalade or apple butter.

SMALL LOAF (1 POUND)	INGREDIENTS	LARGE LOAF (1½ POUNDS)
¾ cup plus 2 tablespoons	milk	1¼ cups
1 teaspoon	active dry yeast	1½ teaspoons
1⅔ cups	bread flour	2½ cups
⅔ cup	rye flour	1 cup
1 teaspoon	salt	1½ teaspoons
½ teaspoon	ground cardamom	¾ teaspoon
3 tablespoons	vegetable oil	¼ cup
2 teaspoons	barley malt syrup*	1 tablespoon
¼ cup	honey	⅓ cup
2	eggs	3

1. Scald the milk. Let cool to room temperature.

2. Add the milk and all remaining ingredients in the order suggested by your bread machine manual and process on the basic bread cycle according to the manufacturer's directions.

* Available in health food stores.

Onion Rye Bread

Chopped onion adds flavor and moisture, making this a bread that will give new life to a sandwich made from last night's leftovers, such as an extra hamburger or salisbury steak, cold roast chicken, or pork. It also goes well with egg or tuna salad, ham and cheese, or in a toasted Swiss cheese sandwich.

SMALL LOAF (1 POUND)	INGREDIENTS	LARGE LOAF (1½ POUNDS)
1¼ teaspoons	active dry yeast	2 teaspoons
1½ cups	bread flour	2¼ cups
½ cup	rye flour	¾ cup
1 tablespoon	sugar	1½ tablespoons
2 tablespoons	powdered milk	3 tablespoons
1 tablespoon	caraway seeds	1½ tablespoons
1 teaspoon	salt	1½ teaspoons
1 tablespoon	vegetable oil	1½ tablespoons
¼ cup	chopped raw onion	⅓ cup
½ cup	sourdough starter (page 7) *	¾ cup
½ cup	water	¾ cup

Add all ingredients in the order suggested by your bread machine manual and process on the basic bread cycle according to the manufacturer's directions. Let cool before slicing. This bread is too moist to eat very warm.

* After measuring out what is needed for this recipe, be sure to replenish your sourdough starter with equal amounts of flour and water.

Potato Rye Bread

This sandwich bread is so moist it can revive dry meat. No one will know you overcooked the roast if you slice it thin and slap it between two mustard-glazed pieces of potato rye bread. Consider putting a thin slice of Swiss cheese and a sliver of apple in the middle, too, and cooking the sandwich just long enough to melt the cheese.

SMALL LOAF (1 POUND)	INGREDIENTS	LARGE LOAF (1½ POUNDS)
1½ teaspoons	active dry yeast	2¼ teaspoons
1½ cups	bread flour	2¼ cups
½ cup	rye flour	¾ cup
1 tablespoon	sugar	1½ tablespoons
1 teaspoon	salt	1½ teaspoons
¼ teaspoon	freshly ground black pepper	½ teaspoon
2 teaspoons	dill seeds	1 tablespoon
2 teaspoons	caraway seeds	1 tablespoon
½ cup	mashed potato	¾ cup
1 cup	buttermilk	1½ cups

Add all ingredients in the order suggested by your bread machine manual and process on the basic bread cycle according to the manufacturer's directions.

Sweet and Sour Spicy Rye Bread

Slice this low, dense rye thin for ham and cheese sandwiches or an open-faced Swiss cheese melt. Slice very thin and bake at 350 degrees for ten minutes to make a tangy melba toast.

SMALL LOAF (1 POUND)	INGREDIENTS	LARGE LOAF (1½ POUNDS)
1½ teaspoons	active dry yeast	2¼ teaspoons
1½ cups	bread flour	2¼ cups
½ cup	rye flour	¾ cup
1 tablespoon	grated orange zest	1½ tablespoons
½ teaspoon	ground ginger	¾ teaspoon
½ teaspoon	ground cloves	¾ teaspoon
½ teaspoon	anise seed	¾ teaspoon
½ teaspoon	salt	¾ teaspoon
1 tablespoon	vegetable oil	1½ tablespoons
¼ cup	honey	⅓ cup
½ cup	sourdough starter (page 7) *	¾ cup
½ cup	water	¾ cup

Add all ingredients in the order suggested by your bread machine manual and process on the basic bread cycle according to the manufacturer's directions.

* After measuring out what is needed for this recipe, be sure to replenish your sourdough starter with equal amounts of flour and water.

Malted Wheat Sandwich Bread

This is a very unthreatening bread for children. They will not even suspect it is healthy. Tuna salad, peanut butter and jelly, bologna are quite at home between the slices, and it makes first-rate toast.

SMALL LOAF (1 POUND)	INGREDIENTS	LARGE LOAF (1½ POUNDS)
1¼ teaspoons	active dry yeast	2 teaspoons
2 cups	bread flour	3 cups
¼ cup	wheat bran	⅓ cup
1 teaspoon	salt	1½ teaspoons
2 tablespoons	vegetable oil	3 tablespoons
1 teaspoon	barley malt syrup*	1½ teaspoons
¾ cup plus 2 tablespoons	water	1¼ cups

Add all ingredients in the order suggested by your bread machine manual and process on the basic bread cycle according to the manufacturer's directions.

* Available in health food stores.

Chapter Two

A Bread for Every Season

Even enthusiastic bread makers rarely bake in summer; the oven creates too much heat. The bread machine changes all that since it does not heat up the kitchen or the baker. The abundant, intensely flavored fruits and vegetables of summer fill bread with the real taste of tomatoes, basil, or blueberries. A bountiful garden calls for a bread machine, so one need not live by salad alone. And bread is so portable —perfect for the beach, hiking, boating, or nibbling in the hammock.

In the fall there are pears and apples ripening too quickly. Adding them raw with their skins intact makes moist, perfumed breads with maximum vitamin content; nothing is lost. In winter potatoes and carrots, onions and garlic, bananas and oranges, dried fruits, and frozen vegetables make fine breads. Orange zest adds wonderful pungency to both sweet and savory loaves. Dried fruits naturally sweeten and help preserve bread.

When the weather is soft and beautiful in spring who wants to be indoors baking bread? No need. Bread flecked with new herbs can be rising and baking in the machine, while you the baker are out biking or gardening in the sunshine.

Artichoke and Cracked Wheat Bread

Paper-thin slices of Italian salami or prosciutto on thin slices of this bread make delicious hors d'oeuvres. Turn those into hearty sandwiches with thicker slices of bread, more cold meats, and some mozzarella cheese. To go with a pasta dinner, serve slices plain or lightly painted with olive oil and toasted under the broiler.

SMALL LOAF (1 POUND)	INGREDIENTS	LARGE LOAF (1½ POUNDS)
6-ounce jar	marinated artichoke hearts	9-ounce jar
2 tablespoons	reserved liquid from jar of artichokes	3 tablespoons
1 teaspoon	active dry yeast	1½ teaspoons
1 cup	bread flour	1½ cups
1 cup	whole wheat flour	1½ cups
¼ cup	cracked wheat	⅓ cup
1 tablespoon	sugar	1½ tablespoons
1 teaspoon	salt	1½ teaspoons
¼ teaspoon	freshly ground black pepper	¼ teaspoon
2 tablespoons	grated Parmesan cheese	3 tablespoons
⅔ cup	warm water	1 cup

1. Drain the marinated artichoke hearts, reserving the liquid.

2. Add the artichoke hearts, reserved marinade, and all remaining ingredients in the order suggested by your bread machine manual and process on the basic bread cycle according to the manufacturer's directions.

Bananas and Cream Bread

Good warm or cool, this mildly sweet bread does well as a coffee cake and as a sandwich bread with cream cheese or cottage cheese filling. Since the ripest bananas make the best bread, you can use up your soft bananas here.

SMALL LOAF (1 POUND)	INGREDIENTS	LARGE LOAF (1½ POUNDS)
1¼ teaspoons	active dry yeast	2 teaspoons
2 cups	bread flour	3 cups
2 tablespoons	wheat germ	3 tablespoons
2 tablespoons	powdered milk	3 tablespoons
1 tablespoon	sugar	1½ tablespoons
1 teaspoon	salt	1½ teaspoons
½ teaspoon	grated nutmeg	¾ teaspoon
1 tablespoon	vegetable oil	1½ tablespoons
¾ cup	mashed ripe banana	1 cup plus 2 tablespoons
½ cup	sour cream or plain yogurt	¾ cup
¼ cup	water	¼ cup plus 1 tablespoon
½ cup	raisins or chopped nuts (optional)	¾ cup

1. Add all ingredients except the raisins or nuts, if included, in the order suggested by your bread machine manual and process on the basic bread cycle according to the manufacturer's directions.

2. At the beeper (or at the end of the first kneading in the Panasonic or National), add the raisins or nuts.

Blueberry and Oat Bread

Take blueberry and oat bread to the beach to watch the sunrise, or eat it for breakfast or as an afternoon snack. Somehow this tastes better outdoors without any adornment; it doesn't even need butter.

SMALL LOAF (1 POUND)	INGREDIENTS	LARGE LOAF (1½ POUNDS)
1½ teaspoons	active dry yeast	2¼ teaspoons
1¾ cups plus 2 tablespoons	bread flour	2¾ cups plus 1 tablespoon
½ cup	rolled oats	¾ cup
2 tablespoons	wheat germ	3 tablespoons
1 tablespoon	vegetable oil	1½ tablespoons
3 tablespoons	brown sugar	¼ cup
1 teaspoon	salt	1½ teaspoons
3 tablespoons	unsalted butter	4 tablespoons
⅔ cup	water	1 cup
¾ cup	blueberries	1 cup

1. Add all ingredients except the blueberries in the order suggested by your bread machine manual and process on the basic bread cycle according to the manufacturer's directions.

2. At the beeper (or at the end of the first kneading in the Panasonic or National), add the blueberries.

Caesar's Sourdough Bread

If Caesar made bread instead of salad dressing, this would be it. Sandwich with lettuce and tomatoes or tuna salad, or serve it with a green salad. For an hors d'oeuvre, toast slices and top with steak tartare or a sliver of rare cooked beef. The crusty ends can be cut into croutons, toasted in a frying pan, and tossed in a salad.

SMALL LOAF (1 POUND)	INGREDIENTS	LARGE LOAF (1½ POUNDS)
1¼ teaspoons	active dry yeast	2½ teaspoons
1⅓ cup	bread flour	2 cups
⅔ cup	whole wheat flour	1 cup
1	garlic clove(s), minced	1½
1 tablespoon	sugar	1½ tablespoons
½ teaspoon	salt	¾ teaspoon
3 tablespoons	grated Parmesan cheese	¼ cup
2 tablespoons	olive oil	3 tablespoons
3	anchovy fillets, chopped	4
1 teaspoon	grated lemon zest	1½ teaspoons
1 cup	sourdough starter (page 7) *	1½ cups
⅓ cup	water	½ cup

Add all ingredients in the order suggested by your bread machine manual and process on the basic bread cycle according to the manufacturer's directions.

* After measuring out what is needed for this recipe, be sure to replenish your sourdough starter with equal amounts of flour and water.

Carrot and Thyme Bread

This moist multi-grain bread is excellent filled with nutted cream cheese, chicken salad, or avocado and sprouts. It is chock full of vitamins and fiber and tastes good with fruit or vegetable salad or lentil or bean soup.

SMALL LOAF (1 POUND)	INGREDIENTS	LARGE LOAF (1½ POUNDS)
1½ teaspoons	active dry yeast	2½ teaspoons
1½ cups	bread flour	2¼ cups
⅔ cup	rye flour	1 cup
⅓ cup	yellow cornmeal	½ cup
1 tablespoon	sugar	1½ tablespoons
1 teaspoon	salt	1½ teaspoons
1 tablespoon	dried thyme leaves	1½ tablespoons
2 tablespoons	vegetable oil	3 tablespoons
1⅓ cups	grated or finely chopped carrots	2 cups
½ cup	water	⅔ cup

Add all ingredients in the order suggested by your bread machine manual and process on the basic bread cycle according to the manufacturer's directions. Let the loaf cool before slicing.

Sweet and Sour Citrus Bread

The sweet and tart citrus flavor of this loaf complements chicken, turkey, and cold roast pork. Toast made from this moist, dense bread has a clear flavor that should not be masked by anything more overbearing than a slim coating of butter or cottage cheese.

SMALL LOAF (1 POUND)	INGREDIENTS	LARGE LOAF (1½ POUNDS)
1¼ teaspoons	active dry yeast	1¾ teaspoons
2 cups	bread flour	3 cups
2 tablespoons	wheat germ	3 tablespoons
2 tablespoons	wheat bran	3 tablespoons
¼ cup	sugar	⅓ cup
1 teaspoon	salt	1½ teaspoons
1½ teaspoons	grated orange zest	2 teaspoons
1 teaspoon	grated lemon zest	1½ teaspoons
1	egg	1
2 tablespoons	unsalted butter	3 tablespoons
½ cup	sourdough starter (page 7) *	¾ cup
½ cup	water	¾ cup

Add all ingredients in the order suggested by your bread machine manual and process on the basic bread cycle according to the manufacturer's directions.

* After measuring out what is needed for this recipe, be sure to replenish your sourdough starter with equal amounts of flour and water.

Grapefruit and Poppy Seed Bread

Could you make a more nutritious, refreshing commuter breakfast than thick slices of this bread either plain or spread with butter, cream cheese, or marmalade? It also makes an unusual but delicious turkey or chicken sandwich.

SMALL LOAF (1 POUND)	INGREDIENTS	LARGE LOAF (1½ POUNDS)
1½ teaspoons	active dry yeast	2¼ teaspoons
1½ cups plus 2 tablespoons	bread flour	2½ cups
2 tablespoons	wheat germ	3 tablespoons
½ cup	wheat bran	¾ cup
2 tablespoons	powdered milk	3 tablespoons
3 tablespoons	poppy seeds	¼ cup
1 tablespoon	sugar	1½ tablespoons
1 teaspoon	salt	1½ teaspoons
2 tablespoons	grated grapefruit zest	3 tablespoons
1 tablespoon	vegetable oil	1½ tablespoons
3 tablespoons	fresh grapefruit juice	¼ cup
⅔ cup	warm water	1 cup

Add all ingredients in the order suggested by your bread machine manual and process on the basic bread cycle according to the manufacturer's directions.

Lemonade Bread

Sweet, but not cloying, and slightly tart, this is good beach food or porch food. If you slice and wrap the bread in your beach towel before you leave home, there will be no paper or plastic wrapper to add to the trash on the beach. Just shake out the crumbs before you dry off.

SMALL LOAF (1 POUND)	INGREDIENTS	LARGE LOAF (1½ POUNDS)
1½ teaspoons	active dry yeast	2½ teaspoons
1¼ cups	bread flour	1¾ cups plus 2 tablespoons
1 cup	whole wheat flour	1½ cups
¾ teaspoon	salt	1¼ teaspoons
1 tablespoon	sugar	1½ tablespoons
1 tablespoon	vegetable oil	1½ tablespoons
⅓ cup	frozen lemonade concentrate, thawed	¼ cup
½ cup plus 2 tablespoons	water	1 cup

Add all ingredients in the order suggested by your bread machine manual and process on the basic bread cycle according to the manufacturer's directions.

Lime and Coconut Milk Bread

A big summer fruit salad tastes even better with the tropical taste of this light bread. Slices are irresistible with nutted cream cheese or chicken salad. Spread with a mashed, ripe mango if you like, but eschew jam, which will hide the subtly sweet but tart taste of the loaf.

SMALL LOAF (1 POUND)	INGREDIENTS	LARGE LOAF (1½ POUNDS)
1½ teaspoons	active dry yeast	2½ teaspoons
1⅓ cups	bread flour	2 cups
¾ cup	whole wheat flour	1¼ cups
3 tablespoons	rolled oats	¼ cup
3 tablespoons	yellow cornmeal	¼ cup
2 tablespoons	sugar	3 tablespoons
1 teaspoon	salt	1½ teaspoons
2 tablespoons	grated lime zest	3 tablespoons
1 tablespoon	vegetable oil	1½ tablespoons
½ cup	flaked coconut	¾ cup
⅓ cup	unsweetened coconut milk	½ cup
⅔ cup	water	1 cup

Add all ingredients in the order suggested by your bread machine manual and process on the basic bread cycle according to the manufacturer's directions.

Minted Pea Bread

Serve this cooling bread with cold creamed soup or gazpacho, with tomato and mozzarella salad, or with cold fish. It is refreshing also with spicy Middle Eastern or Indian food.

SMALL LOAF (1 POUND)	INGREDIENTS	LARGE LOAF (1½ POUNDS)
1 cup	fresh or frozen peas	1½ cups
1¼ teaspoons	active dry yeast	2 teaspoons
2 cups	bread flour	3 cups
2 tablespoons	wheat bran	3 tablespoons
1 tablespoon	sugar	1½ tablespoons
1 teaspoon	salt	1½ teaspoons
¼ teaspoon	freshly ground black pepper	¼ teaspoon
¼ cup	chopped fresh mint leaves	⅓ cup
	or	
1 tablespoon	dried mint	1½ tablespoons
⅔ cup	water	¾ cup plus 2 tablespoons

1. Defrost peas if they are frozen. Puree in a blender or food processor.
2. Add the pureed peas and all remaining ingredients in the order suggested by your bread machine manual and process on the basic bread cycle according to the manufacturer's directions.

Pear and Hazelnut Bread

Ripe, actually overripe, pears make the sweetest, moistest bread. This subtly flavored loaf does fine on its own and makes excellent plain, cinnamon, or French toast. Or place a thin slice of cold cooked lamb on it and warm in the broiler briefly.

SMALL LOAF (1 POUND)	INGREDIENTS	LARGE LOAF (1½ POUNDS)
1 large	ripe pear(s)	1½ large
2 tablespoons	vegetable oil	3 tablespoons
1¼ teaspoons	active dry yeast	1½ teaspoons
1⅓ cups	bread flour	2 cups
¾ cup	rye flour	1 cup plus 2 tablespoons
2 tablespoons	wheat germ	3 tablespoons
1 teaspoon	salt	1½ teaspoons
2 tablespoons	sugar	3 tablespoons
1 teaspoon	fennel seeds	1½ teaspoons
2 tablespoons	chopped hazelnuts	3 tablespoons
⅓ cup	water	½ cup

1. Core and chop the pear(s), leaving the skin on. In a small saucepan cook the chopped pear in the oil over medium-low heat, stirring occasionally, until very soft, about 10 minutes. Let the pear puree cool.

2. Add the pear puree and all remaining ingredients in the order suggested by your bread machine manual and process on the basic bread cycle according to the manufacturer's directions.

Ratatouille Bread

This bread makes a wonderful cold steak or grilled lamb sandwich.

SMALL LOAF (1 POUND)	INGREDIENTS	LARGE LOAF (1½ POUNDS)
¼ cup	chopped yellow (summer) squash	⅓ cup
¼ cup	chopped zucchini	⅓ cup
¼ cup	chopped red or green bell pepper	⅓ cup
2 tablespoons	olive oil	3 tablespoons
1	plum tomato(es)	2
1	garlic clove(s), minced	2
1½ teaspoons	active dry yeast	2¼ teaspoons
2 cups	bread flour	3 cups
¼ cup	wheat bran	⅓ cup
1 teaspoon	sugar	1½ teaspoons
1 teaspoon	salt	1½ teaspoons
1 tablespoon	chopped fresh basil	1½ tablespoons
½ cup	water	¾ cup

1. In a large skillet, cook the yellow squash, zucchini, and bell pepper in olive oil over medium-high heat, stirring often, until barely tender, about 3 minutes. Remove from the heat and let cool. Seed and chop the tomato(es).

2. Add the vegetables and all remaining ingredients in the order suggested by your bread machine manual and process on the basic bread cycle according to the manufacturer's directions.

Sausage, Herb, and Onion Bread

Serve this moist, spicy bread with a crisp green salad or with vegetable soup for a casual après-ski party. The only other thing you need is beer or a hearty red wine.

SMALL LOAF (1 POUND)	INGREDIENTS	LARGE LOAF (1½ POUNDS)
4 ounces	Italian sausage, sweet or hot	6 ounces
1 small	onion, minced	1 medium
1½ teaspoons	active dry yeast	2¼ teaspoons
2 cups	bread flour	3 cups
¼ cup	wheat bran	¼ cup plus 2 tablespoons
1 tablespoon	sugar	1½ tablespoons
1 teaspoon	salt	1½ teaspoons
1 tablespoon	grated Parmesan cheese	1½ tablespoons
½ teaspoon	dried thyme leaves	¾ teaspoon
½ teaspoon	dried rosemary	¾ teaspoon
½ teaspoon	dried oregano	¾ teaspoon
½ teaspoon	dried basil	¾ teaspoon
¾ cup	water	1 cup plus 2 tablespoons

1. Remove the casing from the sausage and crumble the meat into a medium nonstick skillet. Cook over medium heat, stirring to break sausage into small pieces, until it begins to render its juices, about 3 minutes. Add the onion and cook until the sausage is no longer pink and the onion softens, about 5 minutes. Remove from the heat and let cool.

2. Add the cooled sausage and onion and all remaining ingredients in the order suggested by your bread machine manual and process on the basic bread cycle according to the manufacturer's directions.

Semolina Sesame Bread

Semolina flour is the strong, silent type: It has great tear (texture) and character, but a mild flavor that does not announce itself. Its understated nature lets this bread go anywhere with almost anything—alongside an assertive French or Italian sauce, around juicy roast meat, or under ripe cheese.

SMALL LOAF (1 POUND)	INGREDIENTS	LARGE LOAF (1½ POUNDS)
1¼ teaspoons	active dry yeast	2 teaspoons
2 cups	semolina flour	3 cups
2 tablespoons	wheat germ	3 tablespoons
1 tablespoon	sugar	1½ tablespoons
1¼ teaspoons	salt	1½ teaspoons
2 tablespoons	olive oil	3 tablespoons
¼ cup	toasted sesame seeds	⅓ cup
¾ cup plus 2 tablespoons	water	1¼ cups

Add all ingredients in the order suggested by your bread machine manual and process on the basic bread cycle according to the manufacturer's directions.

Summer Fruit Bread

This sweet, moist bread can go to the beach and is also great on a sailboat, a cruise or a race, because it keeps well and does not make too many crumbs. Bread makes good boat food because you can eat it with one hand and still have a hand free to take the tiller.

SMALL LOAF (1 POUND)	INGREDIENTS	LARGE LOAF (1½ POUNDS)
⅓ cup	blueberries or blackberries (fresh or frozen)	½ cup
1½ teaspoons	active dry yeast	2½ teaspoons
1½ cups	bread flour	2¼ cups
⅔ cup	whole wheat flour	1 cup
3 tablespoons	sugar	¼ cup
2 tablespoons	powdered milk	3 tablespoons
¼ teaspoon	ground cloves	½ teaspoon
¼ teaspoon	ground cinnamon	½ teaspoon
¾ teaspoon	salt	1 teaspoon
⅔ cup	chopped fresh ripe peach or nectarine	1 cup
1 tablespoon	unsalted butter	1½ tablespoons
1	egg	1
⅓ cup	water	⅔ cup

1. If the blueberries or blackberries are fresh, freeze them anyway so they will not get too mushy in the bread dough. In some machines they will stay partially solid; in others, berries will marbleize the dough.

2. Add all ingredients except the berries in the order suggested by your bread machine manual and process on the basic bread cycle according to the manufacturer's directions.

3. At the beeper (or at the end of the first kneading in the Panasonic or National), add the berries.

Summer Vegetable Bread

When squash comes into season this vegetable bread can make use of it immediately—for consuming that day—or the bread can be frozen.

SMALL LOAF (1 POUND)	INGREDIENTS	LARGE LOAF (1½ POUNDS)
½ cup	julienned red bell pepper, zucchini, and yellow squash	¾ cup
1½ teaspoons	active dry yeast	2¼ teaspoons
1¼ cups	bread flour	1¾ cups plus 2 tablespoons
½ cup	whole wheat flour	¾ cup
½ cup	wheat bran	¾ cup
1 tablespoon	sugar	1½ tablespoons
¾ teaspoon	salt	1 teaspoon
1 tablespoon	vegetable oil	1½ tablespoons
1 tablespoon	soy sauce	1½ tablespoons
⅔ cup	water	1 cup

1. Cut the vegetables by hand or in a food processor about 30 minutes in advance. Drain on paper towels or in a colander.

2. Add all ingredients except the vegetables in the order suggested by your bread machine manual and process on the basic bread cycle according to the manufacturer's directions.

3. At the beeper (or at the end of the first kneading in the Panasonic or National), add the vegetables.

Spinach and Feta Bread

The green spinach running through this bread makes it look like marble. The loaf is moist yet dense and fragrant with nutmeg and cheese. Meat loaf or cold lamb make excellent sandwich fillings, or eat slices with chicken, egg-lemon, or beef and barley soup.

SMALL LOAF (1 POUND)	INGREDIENTS	LARGE LOAF (1½ POUNDS)
½ cup	frozen chopped spinach	¾ cup
1½ teaspoons	active dry yeast	2¼ teaspoons
2 cups	bread flour	3 cups
¼ cup	wheat bran	⅓ cup
1 tablespoon	sugar	1½ tablespoons
1 teaspoon	salt	1½ teaspoons
1 teaspoon	grated nutmeg	1½ teaspoons
¼ teaspoon	ground black pepper	½ teaspoon
2 tablespoons	vegetable oil	3 tablespoons
1	egg	1
¼ cup	crumbled feta cheese	⅓ cup
⅓ cup	water	½ cup

1. Defrost the spinach overnight in the refrigerator or in a microwave. Do not cook it. Wrap in a dish towel or a piece of clean old sheeting and tighten the fabric around the spinach to squeeze out all the liquid.

2. Add all ingredients in the order suggested by your bread machine manual and process on the basic bread cycle according to the manufacturer's directions. Let the loaf cool before slicing.

Sweet Wine, Apples, and Nut Bread

The flavor of this bread is slightly sweet and mellow. It makes a broiled chicken breast more interesting without overpowering it. The apples are added later to retain maximum flavor.

SMALL LOAF (1 POUND)	INGREDIENTS	LARGE LOAF (1½ POUNDS)
1½ teaspoons	active dry yeast	2½ teaspoons
1½ cups	bread flour	2¼ cups
½ cup	whole wheat flour	¾ cup
1 tablespoon	sugar	1½ tablespoons
½ teaspoon	salt	¾ teaspoon
½ cup	walnut pieces	¾ cup
½ cup	sweet red wine, such as Concord	¾ cup
¼ cup	water	⅓ cup
⅓ cup	chopped apple, skin on	½ cup

1. Add all ingredients except the chopped apple in the order suggested by your bread machine manual and process on the basic bread cycle according to the manufacturer's directions.

2. At the beeper (or at the end of the first kneading in the Panasonic or National), add the apple.

Tabbouleh Bread

Whenever you make tabbouleh salad or buy it at your deli or favorite take-out shop, save some for this very moist and spicy but refreshing bread. It goes particularly well with split pea or lentil soup or with barbecued chicken or lamb.

SMALL LOAF (1 POUND)	INGREDIENTS	LARGE LOAF (1½ POUNDS)
1½ teaspoons	active dry yeast	2¼ teaspoons
1⅔ cups	bread flour	2⅔ cups
1 teaspoon	salt	1½ teaspoons
¼ teaspoon	ground black pepper	½ teaspoon
¾ cup	tabbouleh	1 cup plus 2 tablespoons
¾ cup plus 2 tablespoons	water	1⅓ cups

Add all ingredients in the order suggested by your bread machine manual and process on the basic bread cycle according to the manufacturer's directions. Let the loaf cool before slicing.

Tomato Sourdough Bread

Toasted cheese sandwiches are outstanding on this bread. Use Cheddar or mozzarella, or be adventurous and try havarti or gorgonzola or fontina. When fresh herbs are in season, sprinkle chopped fresh basil or rosemary on the cheese before you add the top slice of bread and grill the sandwich.

SMALL LOAF (1 POUND)	INGREDIENTS	LARGE LOAF (1½ POUNDS)
1¼ teaspoons	active dry yeast	2¼ teaspoons
1¾ cups plus 2 tablespoons	bread flour	2¾ cups plus 1 tablespoon
1 tablespoon	sugar	1½ tablespoons
1 teaspoon	salt	1½ teaspoons
2 tablespoons	vegetable oil	3 tablespoons
2 tablespoons	tomato paste	3 tablespoons
1 tablespoon	chopped onions	1½ tablespoons
1 tablespoon	vinegar	1½ tablespoons
¼ cup	sourdough starter (page 7) *	⅓ cup
½ cup plus 2 tablespoons	water	¾ cup plus 1 tablespoon

Add all ingredients in the order suggested by your bread machine manual and process on the basic bread cycle according to the manufacturer's directions. Let the loaf cool before slicing.

* After measuring out what is needed for this recipe, be sure to replenish your sourdough starter with equal amounts of flour and water.

Walnut and Apricot White Bread

Both chopped walnuts and walnut oil flavor this subtle bread, whose sweetness is derived almost completely from dried apricots. It makes very sophisticated toast to go with scrambled eggs or an omelet. Late on a rainy, cold night, enjoy a slice with a big mug of cocoa.

SMALL LOAF (1 POUND)	INGREDIENTS	LARGE LOAF (1½ POUNDS)
1¼ teaspoons	active dry yeast	2 teaspoons
2 cups	bread flour	3 cups
1 tablespoon	sugar	1½ tablespoons
1 teaspoon	salt	1½ teaspoons
½ cup	chopped walnuts	¾ cup
1 tablespoon	walnut oil * or vegetable oil	1½ tablespoons
¾ cup plus 1 tablespoon	water	1¼ cups
¼ cup	dried apricots	⅓ cup

1. Add all ingredients except the apricots in the order suggested by your bread machine manual and process on the basic bread cycle according to the manufacturer's directions.

2. With a kitchen scissors, snip the apricots into ¼-inch pieces. At the beeper (or at the end of the first kneading in the Panasonic or National), add the apricots. Eat warm, cool, or toasted.

* Be sure to store walnut oil in the refrigerator, or it will turn rancid quickly.

Vanilla Walnut Coffee Cake

Friends and relatives of all ages will enjoy this rich bread for dessert or for breakfast. A highly aromatic loaf, it will make your whole kitchen smell wonderful for hours.

SMALL LOAF (1 POUND)	INGREDIENTS	LARGE LOAF (1½ POUNDS)
⅔ cup	milk	1 cup
2 tablespoons	butter	3 tablespoons
3 tablespoons	honey	¼ cup
1½ teaspoons	active dry yeast	2¼ teaspoons
1½ cups	bread flour	2¼ cups
¾ teaspoon	salt	1 teaspoon
1 teaspoon	vanilla extract	1½ teaspoons
1	whole egg(s)	2
1	egg yolk	1
2 tablespoons	brown sugar	3 tablespoons
½ cup	chopped walnuts	¾ cup

1. Scald the milk. Stir in the butter and honey and let cool to room temperature.

2. Add the milk mixture and all remaining ingredients except the brown sugar and walnuts in the order suggested by your bread machine manual and process on the basic bread cycle according to the manufacturer's directions.

3. At the beeper (or at the end of the first kneading in the Panasonic or National), add the brown sugar and walnuts. Eat warm or cool.

Winter Fruit Bread

Slice this very moist, mildly sweet bread thin and spread with nutted or plain cream cheese for tea sandwiches. Allow thicker slices for curried chicken salad or roast turkey sandwiches.

SMALL LOAF (1 POUND)	INGREDIENTS	LARGE LOAF (1½ POUNDS)
1½ teaspoons	active dry yeast	2¼ teaspoons
1¼ cups	bread flour	2 cups
1 cup	whole wheat flour	1½ cups
1 tablespoon	sugar	1½ tablespoons
1 teaspoon	salt	1½ teaspoons
1 tablespoon	grated orange zest	1½ tablespoons
¼ cup	chopped raisins or currants	⅓ cup
¼ cup	applesauce	⅓ cup
¼ cup	mashed banana	⅓ cup
⅛ teaspoon	ground cloves	¼ teaspoon
⅛ teaspoon	ground cinnamon	¼ teaspoon
1 tablespoon	vegetable oil	1½ tablespoons
⅔ cup	water	1 cup

Add all ingredients in the order suggested by your bread machine manual and process on the basic bread cycle according to the manufacturer's directions. Let the loaf cool completely before eating. This bread tastes even better the next day.

Winter Vegetable Bread

This bread is pink outside and golden within, flecked with red and orange—color and flavor that will brighten up any dreary winter day. Cold meat, such as roast beef or ham, fills these slices very well. The bread also tastes good with beef and barley soup or beef stew.

SMALL LOAF (1 POUND)	INGREDIENTS	LARGE LOAF (1½ POUNDS)
1¼ teaspoons	active dry yeast	2 teaspoons
1¼ cups	bread flour	1¾ cups plus 2 tablespoons
2 tablespoons	rolled oats	3 tablespoons
1 cup	whole wheat flour	1½ cups
1 teaspoon	ground ginger	1½ teaspoons
1 tablespoon	sugar	1½ tablespoons
1 teaspoon	salt	1½ teaspoons
1 tablespoon	vegetable oil	1½ teaspoons
½ cup	water	¾ cup
½ cup	grated carrots	¾ cup
½ cup	chopped canned beets	¾ cup

1. Add all ingredients except the carrots and beets in the order suggested by your bread machine manual and process on the basic bread cycle according to the manufacturer's directions.

2. At the beeper (or at the end of the first kneading in the Panasonic or National), add the carrots and beets.

Yogurt and Pumpkin Bread

If you like pumpkin pie, you will enjoy the lightly spiced pumpkin flavor of this protein-rich bread, full of nuggets of raisins and nuts. Serve for breakfast or take it along when you venture out to watch the turning of the leaves or the soccer matches.

SMALL LOAF (1 POUND)	INGREDIENTS	LARGE LOAF (1½ POUNDS)
1½ teaspoons	active dry yeast	2 teaspoons
2 cups	bread flour	3 cups
2 tablespoons	wheat germ	3 tablespoons
2 tablespoons	powdered milk	3 tablespoons
2 tablespoons	sugar	3 tablespoons
¼ teaspoon	ground ginger	½ teaspoon
½ teaspoon	ground cinnamon	¾ teaspoon
1 teaspoon	salt	1½ teaspoons
¾ cup	canned pumpkin	1 cup plus 2 tablespoons
¼ cup	plain yogurt	⅓ cup
¼ cup	water	⅓ cup
¼ cup	chopped pecans	⅓ cup
¼ cup	raisins	⅓ cup

1. Add all ingredients except the pecans and raisins in the order suggested by your bread machine manual and process on the basic bread cycle according to the manufacturer's directions.

2. At the beeper (or at the end of the first kneading in the Panasonic or National), add the pecans and raisins.

Zucchini Nut and Raisin Bread

Is it August, and your garden is producing so many zucchini you do not know what to do with them? Your friends don't want any, because they are bringing you zucchini from their gardens. Make this raisin and/or nut-studded sweet bread with even big zucchini. Serve for breakfast or snacks.

SMALL LOAF (1 POUND)	INGREDIENTS	LARGE LOAF (1½ POUNDS)
½ cup	grated zucchini	¾ cup
1½ teaspoons	salt	2 teaspoons
1¼ teaspoons	active dry yeast	2 teaspoons
2 cups	bread flour	3 cups
¼ cup	rolled oats	⅓ cup
2 tablespoons	cracked wheat	3 tablespoons
2 tablespoons	powdered milk	3 tablespoons
3 tablespoons	sugar	¼ cup
1 teaspoon	ground cinnamon	1½ teaspoons
½ teaspoon	grated nutmeg	¾ teaspoon
2 tablespoons	vegetable oil	3 tablespoons
1	whole egg	1
0	egg yolk	1
⅓ cup	water	½ cup
½ cup	raisins and/or nuts	¾ cup

1. Put grated zucchini in a colander or strainer. Sprinkle with half the salt, let drain for 30 minutes, and squeeze dry.

2. Add all ingredients except the raisins and/or nuts in the order suggested by your bread machine manual and process on the basic bread cycle according to the manufacturer's directions.

3. At the beeper (or at the end of the first kneading in the Panasonic or National), add the raisins and/or nuts. Let the loaf cool before slicing.

Chapter Three

Whole Grain, Multi-Grain, and Salt-Free Breads

What other food lets you pack it with so much fiber and protein, so many vitamins and minerals as bread? Some of the recipes in this chapter are rich in calcium for young athletes and senior citizens. Others are plump with seeds, nuts, and raisins to energize hikers, bikers, and young mothers. The fat-free and sugar-free breads are good for dieters, in moderation, because they are filling and filled with nutrients. Slice thinly and avoid butter or margarine. Spread with sugar-free jams, low-fat ricotta or cottage cheese, or ripe fruit.

Whole grain breads are chewier and have more fiber and bulk, which makes them more filling and more satisfying. They need less meat or cheese to make a sandwich, and leave you too full for potatoes with your eggs. Whole grain bread encourages healthier eating.

A bread machine lets you add a percentage of fruits, nuts, and whole grains that would be next to impossible to knead in by hand without very big muscles. The low gluten content of most whole grains and their flours makes sticky, hard-to-handle doughs that bake into crunchy, naturally sweetened, moist breads.

Instead of a daily dose of fiber sitting soggily in a cereal bowl, these high-fiber breads are served in tweedy slices that age and travel well. Once the pantry is stocked from a health food store or mail-order catalog, these breads will become basic in your kitchen bakery.

Anadama Bread

There are two reasons why this old recipe appears with some variation in so many cookbooks: it is wholesome, and it tastes good. Such hearty taste and texture are made for morning toast and for tuna or chicken salad sandwiches.

SMALL LOAF (1 POUND)	INGREDIENTS	LARGE LOAF (1½ POUNDS)
1½ teaspoons	active dry yeast	2¼ teaspoons
1 cup plus 2 tablespoons	bread flour	1⅔ cups
1 cup	whole wheat flour	1½ cups
¼ cup	yellow cornmeal	⅓ cup
¼ cup	unsulphured molasses	⅓ cup
1 teaspoon	salt	1½ teaspoons
1 tablespoon	vegetable oil	1½ tablespoons
1 cup	water	1½ cups

Add all ingredients in the order suggested by your bread machine manual and process on the basic bread cycle according to the manufacturer's directions. Let the loaf cool before slicing.

Barley and Oat Bread

A moist and chewy loaf like this one makes good peanut butter, tuna, or fresh ham sandwiches, and excellent toast. It goes well with vegetable and meat soups, especially Scotch broth.

SMALL LOAF (1 POUND)	INGREDIENTS	LARGE LOAF (1½ POUNDS)
1½ teaspoons	active dry yeast	2¼ teaspoons
1⅔ cups	bread flour	2½ cups
½ cup	barley flour	¾ cup
¼ cup	rolled oats	⅓ cup
2 tablespoons	wheat germ	3 tablespoons
2 tablespoons	powdered milk	3 tablespoons
2 tablespoons	grated orange zest	3 tablespoons
2 tablespoons	sesame seeds (optional)	3 tablespoons
1 teaspoon	salt	1½ teaspoons
2 tablespoons	honey	3 tablespoons
1 tablespoon	vegetable oil	1½ tablespoons
¾ cup plus 2 tablespoons	water	1⅓ cups

Add all ingredients in the order suggested by your bread machine manual and process on the basic bread cycle according to the manufacturer's directions. Eat warm—but not hot—or cool.

Bran and Raisin Bread

This high-standing, light, fragrant loaf provides fiber and fruit when toasted for breakfast. It also brings out the best in peanut or apple butter, cream cheese, and egg or chicken salad.

SMALL LOAF (1 POUND)	INGREDIENTS	LARGE LOAF (1½ POUNDS)
1½ teaspoons	active dry yeast	2¼ teaspoons
1¾ cups plus 2 tablespoons	bread flour	2¾ cups plus 1 tablespoon
⅔ cup	wheat bran	1 cup
2 tablespoons	cracked wheat	3 tablespoons
1 teaspoon	salt	1½ teaspoons
2 teaspoons	grated orange zest	1 tablespoon
1 tablespoon	vegetable oil	1½ tablespoons
1 tablespoon	honey	1½ tablespoons
¾ cup plus 2 tablespoons	water	1¼ cups
¼ cup	raisins or currants	⅓ cup

1. Add all ingredients except the raisins or currants in the order suggested by your bread machine manual and process on the basic bread cycle according to the manufacturer's directions.

2. At the beeper (or at the end of the first kneading in the Panasonic or National), add the raisins or currants. Let the loaf cool before slicing.

Buckwheat and Banana Bread

Raisins add sweetness, moistness, and iron to bread already rich in potassium, protein, and fiber. A few slices make a worthwhile breakfast on the run. This is one of the few breads that is even better the next day.

SMALL LOAF (1 POUND)	INGREDIENTS	LARGE LOAF (1½ POUNDS)
1½ teaspoons	active dry yeast	2¼ teaspoons
1¼ cups	bread flour	2 cups
1 cup	whole wheat flour	1½ cups
½ cup	buckwheat	¾ cup
2 tablespoons	powdered milk	3 tablespoons
1 teaspoon	salt	1½ teaspoons
1 tablespoon	vegetable oil	1½ tablespoons
1 tablespoon	honey	1½ tablespoons
¼ cup	mashed banana	⅓ cup
¼ cup	coarsely chopped raisins	⅓ cup
¾ cup plus 2 tablespoons	water	1¼ cups

Add all ingredients in the order suggested by your bread machine manual and process on the basic bread cycle according to the manufacturer's directions.

Buckwheat, Sesame, and Walnut Bread

Here is a dense, intense bread for buckwheat lovers. It is best eaten cool, in thin slices, and spread sparingly with cream cheese or butter. To serve as an hors d'oeuvre, top with caviar or anchovies; for breakfast, spread with apple butter or your favorite jam.

SMALL LOAF (1 POUND)	INGREDIENTS	LARGE LOAF (1½ POUNDS)
1½ teaspoons	active dry yeast	2¼ teaspoons
½ cup	buckwheat flour	¾ cup
1½ cups	bread flour	2¼ cups
½ cup	whole wheat flour	¾ cup
1 tablespoon	brown sugar	1½ tablespoons
1 teaspoon	salt	1½ teaspoons
1 tablespoon	vegetable oil	1½ tablespoons
2 tablespoons	sesame seeds	3 tablespoons
¼ cup	walnut pieces	⅓ cup
½ cup	sourdough starter (page 7) *	¾ cup
½ cup plus 2 tablespoons	water	¾ cup plus 3 tablespoons

Add all ingredients in the order suggested by your bread machine manual and process on the basic bread cycle according to the manufacturer's directions.

* After measuring out what is needed for this recipe, be sure to replenish your sourdough starter with equal amounts of flour and water.

Bulgur Wheat and Dill Bread

Hearty soups, such as borscht, stand up to this moist bread. It makes a great meat loaf or pot roast sandwich.

SMALL LOAF (1 POUND)	INGREDIENTS	LARGE LOAF (1½ POUNDS)
1½ teaspoons	active dry yeast	2¼ teaspoons
1¾ cups	bread flour	2⅔ cups
½ cup	whole wheat flour	¾ cup
¼ cup	bulgur wheat	¼ cup plus 2 tablespoons
¼ cup	chopped fresh dill	⅓ cup
	or	
1 tablespoon	dried dill weed	1½ tablespoons
1 teaspoon	salt	1½ teaspoons
1 tablespoon	vegetable oil	1½ tablespoons
1 tablespoon	honey	1½ tablespoons
¾ cup plus 2 tablespoons	water	1¼ cups

Add all ingredients in the order suggested by your bread machine manual and process on the basic bread cycle according to the manufacturer's directions.

Sweet Carrot, Raisin, and Nut Bread

This loaf is a lot like carrot cake—high, crumbly, and moist, with an affinity for whipped cream and cream cheese.

SMALL LOAF (1 POUND)	INGREDIENTS	LARGE LOAF (1½ POUNDS)
1½ teaspoons	active dry yeast	2¼ teaspoons
1¾ cups plus 1 tablespoon	bread flour	2¾ cups
½ cup	rye flour	¾ cup
¼ cup	sugar	¼ cup plus 2 tablespoons
1 teaspoon	salt	1½ teaspoons
1 teaspoon	ground ginger	1½ teaspoons
1 teaspoon	ground cinnamon	1½ teaspoons
2 tablespoons	vegetable oil	3 tablespoons
1	egg	1
1½ cups	finely chopped or grated carrots	2¼ cups
¼ cup	water	⅓ cup
¼ cup	raisins	⅓ cup
¼ cup	chopped walnuts	⅓ cup

1. Add all ingredients except the raisins and walnuts in the order suggested by your bread machine manual and process on the basic bread cycle according to the manufacturer's directions.

2. At the beeper (or at the end of the first kneading in the Panasonic or National), add the raisins and nuts.

Milk Chocolate Raisin Bread

If it takes chocolate to get the kids to eat wheat bran and germ, so be it. The chocolate/brown sugar combination creates a cookielike taste, but the texture is airy. This loaf is a real child pleaser.

SMALL LOAF (1 POUND)	INGREDIENTS	LARGE LOAF (1½ POUNDS)
¾ cup plus 2 tablespoons	water	1¼ cups
3 tablespoons	unsweetened cocoa powder	¼ cup
1½ teaspoons	active dry yeast	2½ teaspoons
1¾ cups	bread flour	2⅔ cups
3 tablespoons	wheat germ	¼ cup
3 tablespoons	wheat bran	¼ cup
¼ cup	brown sugar	¼ cup plus 2 tablespoons
2 tablespoons	powdered milk	3 tablespoons
1 teaspoon	salt	1½ teaspoons
1 tablespoon	vegetable oil	1½ tablespoons
½ cup	raisins	¾ cup

1. Bring the water to a boil. Add the cocoa powder and stir until dissolved. Let cool to room temperature.

2. Add the cocoa and all remaining ingredients except the raisins in the order suggested by your bread machine manual and process on the basic bread cycle according to the manufacturer's directions.

3. At the beeper (or at the end of the first kneading in the Panasonic or National), add the raisins. This loaf is best warm, but good cool, too.

Cottage Cheese and Dill Bread

Cottage cheese and powdered milk add calcium to this bread, which also boasts the crunch of cracked wheat and the lively taste of caraway and dill seeds. Roast meat or poultry or cold fish salad make good sandwich fillings for this loaf.

SMALL LOAF (1 POUND)	INGREDIENTS	LARGE LOAF (1½ POUNDS)
1¼ teaspoons	active dry yeast	1¾ teaspoons
2 cups	bread flour	3 cups
2 tablespoons	wheat germ	3 tablespoons
2 tablespoons	cracked wheat	3 tablespoons
2 tablespoons	powdered milk	3 tablespoons
1 tablespoon	sugar	1½ tablespoons
½ teaspoon	salt	1 teaspoon
1 teaspoon	caraway seeds	1½ teaspoons
1 teaspoon	dill seeds	1½ teaspoons
½ cup	cottage cheese	¾ cup
½ cup plus 2 tablespoons	water	1 cup

Add all ingredients in the order suggested by your bread machine manual and process on the basic bread cycle according to the manufacturer's directions.

Cranberry and Wheatberry Bread

Wheatberries give this bread crunch and cranberries make it tart. Chicken or egg salad with good mayonnaise belongs between the slices. It takes about an hour to cook the wheatberries, so anticipate additional time for the making of this bread.

SMALL LOAF (1 POUND)	INGREDIENTS	LARGE LOAF (1½ POUNDS)
2 tablespoons	wheatberries	¼ cup
1½ teaspoons	active dry yeast	2¼ teaspoons
1¼ cups	bread flour	1¾ cups plus 2 tablespoons
1 cup	whole wheat flour	1½ cups
2 tablespoons	sugar	3 tablespoons
1 teaspoon	salt	1½ teaspoons
¼ cup	raisins	⅓ cup
1 tablespoon	vegetable oil	1½ tablespoons
¼ cup	cranberries	⅓ cup
¾ cup	water	1 cup plus 2 tablespoons

1. Cook the wheatberries in 4 times their quantity of water. Bring the water to a boil, then add the wheatberries. Lower the heat and simmer for about 1 hour, until the berries have absorbed the water and are chewy/tender.

2. Add the cooked wheatberries and all remaining ingredients in the order suggested by your bread machine manual and process on the basic bread cycle according to the manufacturer's directions.

Granola Raisin Bread

This bread is nutty, chewy, moist, a little sweet, full of a lot of good things like nuts, fruits, grains, proteins, and vitamins. Spread with peanut butter or apple butter, or tart and sugar-free fruit spreads.

SMALL LOAF (1 POUND)	INGREDIENTS	LARGE LOAF (1½ POUNDS)
1½ teaspoons	active dry yeast	2½ teaspoons
1½ cups	bread flour	2¼ cups
⅔ cup	whole wheat flour	1 cup
2 tablespoons	powdered milk	3 tablespoons
1 teaspoon	salt	1½ teaspoons
1 tablespoon	vegetable oil	1½ tablespoons
1 tablespoon	honey	1½ tablespoons
¾ cup plus 2 tablespoons	water	1¼ cups
⅓ cup	granola	½ cup
¼ cup	raisins	⅓ cup

1. Add all ingredients except the granola and raisins in the order suggested by your bread machine manual and process on the basic bread cycle according to the manufacturer's directions.

2. At the buzzer (or at the end of the first kneading in the Panasonic or National), add the granola and raisins. This bread is good warm or cold.

Fruited Sourdough and Bran Bread

Raisins and dried cherries add another dimension to this bread that already has a complex flavor. It becomes sweet, sour, and nutty and is best enjoyed on its own, with just a smear of butter or cream cheese.

SMALL LOAF (1 POUND)	INGREDIENTS	LARGE LOAF (1½ POUNDS)
1 teaspoon	active dry yeast	1½ teaspoons
1¾ cups	bread flour	2⅔ cups
¼ cup	wheat bran	⅓ cup
1 tablespoon	sugar	1½ tablespoons
1 teaspoon	salt	1½ teaspoons
¾ cup	sourdough starter (page 7) *	1 cup plus 2 tablespoons
½ cup	water	¾ cup
¼ cup	golden raisins	⅓ cup
¼ cup	dried tart cherries	⅓ cup

1. Add all ingredients except the raisins and cherries in the order suggested by your bread machine manual and process on the basic bread cycle according to the manufacturer's directions.

2. At the beeper (or at the end of the first kneading in the Panasonic or National), add the raisins and dried cherries. Let the loaf cool before slicing.

* After measuring out what is needed for this recipe, be sure to replenish your sourdough starter with equal amounts of flour and water.

Sourdough Wheatberries and Walnuts

This bread was inspired by Amy Scherber's recipe in New York Magazine *for a dense bread that required 24 hours of rising and several kneadings. My lighter version tastes good with apricot jam or orange marmalade or goat cheese. Do not toast it; the wheatberries will get too hard.*

SMALL LOAF (1 POUND)	INGREDIENTS	LARGE LOAF (1½ POUNDS)
¼ cup	cooked wheatberries (see step 1)	⅓ cup
1¼ teaspoons	active dry yeast	1¾ teaspoons
1½ cups	bread flour	2¼ cups
⅔ cup	whole wheat flour	1 cup
1 teaspoon	salt	1½ teaspoons
1 tablespoon	vegetable oil	1½ tablespoons
1 tablespoon	honey	1½ tablespoons
½ cup	sourdough starter (page 7) *	¾ cup
½ cup plus 2 tablespoons	water	¾ cup plus 3 tablespoons
¼ cup	chopped walnuts	⅓ cup

1. Cook the wheatberries in 4 times their quantity of water. Bring the water to a boil, then add the wheatberries. Lower the heat and simmer for 1 hour, or until tender; drain. If this is done a day ahead, cover the cooked berries well.

2. Add the cooked wheatberries and all remaining ingredients except the walnuts in the order suggested by your bread machine manual and process on the basic bread cycle according to the manufacturer's directions.

3. At the beeper (or at the end of the first kneading in the Panasonic or National), add the walnuts.

* After measuring out what is needed for this recipe, be sure to replenish your sourdough starter with equal amounts of flour and water.

Sprouted Wheat Bread

Protein and vitamins abound in this light, nutty loaf. It's good for sandwiches or toast. This bread brings out the botanist in each of us. It does not take a lot of time, in total, just some planning:

Three days before you plan to make the bread, start sprouting the berries. Watching children watch the dry little berries turn into living plants is exciting. Add 1 quart of water to ¼ cup wheatberries in a 1½-quart glass or plastic container. Cover with cheesecloth or clean, thin cotton fabric held on with a rubber band and let the container stand in a dark place overnight. Pour the water off through the fabric. Add fresh water, swish it around gently, and pour it off again. Repeat twice a day until the berry sprouts are as long as the berries. The whole process takes 2 to 3 days.

SMALL LOAF (1 POUND)	INGREDIENTS	LARGE LOAF (1½ POUNDS)
1¼ teaspoons	active dry yeast	2 tablespoons
1¼ cups	bread flour	1¾ cups plus 2 tablespoons
1 cup	whole wheat flour	1½ cups
2 tablespoons	powdered milk	3 tablespoons
1 teaspoon	salt	1½ teaspoons
1 tablespoon	vegetable oil	1½ tablespoons
1 tablespoon	honey	1½ tablespoons
¾ cup	water	1 cup plus 2 tablespoons
½ cup	sprouted wheatberries (see headnote)	¾ cup

1. Add all ingredients except the wheatberries in the order suggested by your bread machine manual and process on the basic bread cycle according to the manufacturer's directions.

2. At the beeper (or at the end of the first kneading in the Panasonic or National), add the sprouted wheatberries.

One Hundred Percent Whole Wheat Bread

Bread made entirely from whole wheat is a little flatter than bread made with bread flour, but it has more fiber and vitamins and a sturdy, not too dense texture. Grated orange zest revs up the flavor for a good ham and cheese or club sandwich.

SMALL LOAF (1 POUND)	INGREDIENTS	LARGE LOAF (1½ POUNDS)
½ cup	milk	¾ cup
2 tablespoons	molasses	3 tablespoons
1 tablespoon	unsalted butter	1½ tablespoons
1 teaspoon	active dry yeast	1½ teaspoons
2½ cups	whole wheat flour	3¾ cups
1 tablespoon	grated orange zest	1½ tablespoons
1 teaspoon	salt	1½ teaspoons
½ cup	water	¾ cup

Add all ingredients in the order suggested by your bread machine manual and process on the basic bread cycle according to the manufacturer's directions.

Whole Wheat Swiss Cheese Bread

A crisp crust envelops this moist bread studded with holes left by melted Swiss cheese. It is okay to use leftover cheese in your fridge, those last bits that are a little dry, as long as they aren't moldy. Slices of this bread make sensational sandwiches with lettuce, tomato, sprouts, and scallions—or with just ham. For an hors d'oeuvre: Slice bread thin, cover with mustard and thinly sliced ham, roll up, and cut into pinwheels.

SMALL LOAF (1 POUND)	INGREDIENTS	LARGE LOAF (1½ POUNDS)
1½ teaspoons	active dry yeast	2¼ teaspoons
1 cup plus 2 tablespoons	bread flour	1⅔ cups
½ cup	whole wheat flour	¾ cup
½ cup	cracked wheat flour	¾ cup
2 tablespoons	powdered milk	3 tablespoons
1 tablespoon	sugar	1½ tablespoons
¾ teaspoon	salt	1¼ teaspoons
1 tablespoon	vegetable oil	1½ tablespoons
1 tablespoon	very sharp mustard	1½ tablespoons
¾ cup plus 2 tablespoons	water	1¼ cups
½ cup	grated Swiss cheese	¾ cup

Add all ingredients in the order suggested by your bread machine manual and process on the basic bread cycle according to the manufacturer's directions. Eat warm or cool.

Oat Bread with Pecans and Brown Sugar

Healthful without being heavy and just sweet enough to appeal to children as well as adults, this oat bread is wonderful warm or cooled and toasted.

SMALL LOAF (1 POUND)	INGREDIENTS	LARGE LOAF (1½ POUNDS)
1½ teaspoons	active dry yeast	2¼ teaspoons
1¼ cups	bread flour	1¾ cups plus 2 tablespoons
¼ cup	soy flour*	⅓ cup
½ cup	rolled oats	¾ cup
2 tablespoons	powdered milk	3 tablespoons
¼ cup	cracked wheat	⅓ cup
1 tablespoon	sugar	1½ tablespoons
1 teaspoon	salt	1½ teaspoons
1 tablespoon	vegetable oil	1½ tablespoons
¾ cup plus 2 tablespoons	water	1¼ cups
½ cup	chopped pecans	¾ cup
2 tablespoons	brown sugar	3 tablespoons

1. Add all ingredients except the pecans and brown sugar in the order suggested by your bread machine manual and process on the basic bread cycle according to the manufacturer's directions.

2. Toss the pecans and brown sugar together. At the beeper (or at the end of the first kneading in the Panasonic or National), add the pecans and brown sugar.

* Available in health food stores.

Orange Cinnamon Oatmeal Bread

This moist, flavorful whole grain bread travels well. Sandwich it with fillings like nutted cream cheese, sliced leftover roast chicken, or baked ham and pack it in lunch boxes or back packs. For breakfast, serve with fruit and yogurt or alongside scrambled eggs.

SMALL LOAF (1 POUND)	INGREDIENTS	LARGE LOAF (1½ POUNDS)
1½ teaspoons	active dry yeast	2¼ teaspoons
1 cup plus 2 tablespoons	bread flour	1⅔ cups
½ cup	whole wheat flour	¾ cup
½ cup	rolled oats	¾ cup
2 tablespoons	wheat germ	3 tablespoons
2 tablespoons	powdered milk	3 tablespoons
1 teaspoon	ground cinnamon	1½ teaspoons
1 tablespoon	grated orange zest	1½ tablespoons
2 tablespoons	vegetable oil	3 tablespoons
2 tablespoons	honey	3 tablespoons
½ teaspoon	salt	¾ teaspoon
¾ cup plus 2 tablespoons	water	1⅓ cups

Add all ingredients in the order suggested by your bread machine manual and process on the basic bread cycle according to the manufacturer's directions.

Orange and Honey Salt-Free Bread

If you cannot or prefer not to eat salt, you can still enjoy delicious bread. This fragrant loaf tinged with orange makes excellent sandwiches and toast, and complements gazpacho and hot or cold creamed vegetable soups. Chicken salad, turkey, cold roast beef, or pork with sharp mustard are good fillings.

SMALL LOAF (1 POUND)	INGREDIENTS	LARGE LOAF (1½ POUNDS)
¾ cup plus 2 tablespoons	milk	1¼ cups
2 tablespoons	unsalted butter	3 tablespoons
1½ tablespoons	honey	2 tablespoons
¾ teaspoon	active dry yeast	1⅛ teaspoons
2 cups	bread flour	3 cups
1 tablespoon	grated orange zest	1½ tablespoons

1. Scald the milk. Stir in the butter and honey. Let cool to room temperature.

2. Add the milk mixture and all remaining ingredients in the order suggested by your bread machine manual and process on the basic bread cycle according to the manufacturer's directions.

Salt-Free Tuscan Bread

In Florence this is the bread they use for crostini, toasted slices usually spread with liver pâté, or bruschetta when the rounds are rubbed with garlic and topped with chopped tomato. At first it tastes bland, but it is perfect as a foil for salty or highly flavored foods like prosciutto or anchovies. The more you eat, the better it tastes—with summer tomatoes or cheese, or toasted with a slice of melon. In Italy this bread would not contain any sugar; its deep brown crust would come from the very hot oven. I have added a smidgeon to help the bread become golden.

Since salt is a preservative, this is not a long-lasting bread. After 12 hours, use it only toasted. For bruschetta, toast a thick slice of Tuscan bread, drizzle with olive oil, and rub with a cut garlic clove and top with a generous coat of chopped tomato. For crostini, toast slightly thinner slices and spread with liver pâté.

SMALL LOAF (1 POUND)	INGREDIENTS	LARGE LOAF (1½ POUNDS)
1 teaspoon	active dry yeast	1¾ teaspoons
2 cups	bread flour	3 cups
1 tablespoon	sugar	1½ tablespoons
½ cup	sourdough starter (page 7) *	¾ cup
½ cup	water	¾ cup

Add all ingredients in the order suggested by your bread machine manual and process on the basic bread cycle according to the manufacturer's directions.

* After measuring out what is needed for this recipe, be sure to replenish your sourdough starter with equal amounts of flour and water.

Quinoa Bread

Quinoa (pronounced keen wa) *is an ancient South American high-protein grain recently popularized in the United States. This pearly, nutty grain adds texture and nutritional value to a bread that makes good toast or sandwiches with tuna, cold meat, or an assertive cheese.*

SMALL LOAF (1 POUND)	INGREDIENTS	LARGE LOAF (1½ POUNDS)
¼ cup	quinoa grain	¼ cup plus 2 tablespoons
1½ teaspoons	active dry yeast	2¼ teaspoons
1 cup	bread flour	1½ cups
1 cup	whole wheat flour	1½ cups
1 teaspoon	salt	1½ teaspoons
2 tablespoons	powdered milk	3 tablespoons
¼ teaspoon	ground cloves	¼ teaspoon
1 tablespoon	vegetable oil	1½ tablespoons
2 tablespoons	honey	3 tablespoons
¾ cup	water	1 cup

1. To cook quinoa, add it to twice its measure of boiling water. Simmer for 10 minutes. Drain off any excess liquid and let cool.

2. Add the cooked quinoa and all remaining ingredients in the order suggested by your bread machine manual and process on the basic bread cycle according to the manufacturer's directions.

Triticale Bread

Triticale is a nutritious grain that is a hybrid of wheat and rye. You can find it in most health food stores. It adds to the taste but not much to the rising of bread. In combination with wheat flour, it makes good bread for sandwiches or toast, with a pleasant but unobtrusive flavor.

SMALL LOAF (1 POUND)	INGREDIENTS	LARGE LOAF (1½ POUNDS)
1½ teaspoons	active dry yeast	2½ teaspoons
1⅔ cups	bread flour	2½ cups
¼ cup	soy flour*	⅓ cup
⅔ cup	triticale flour*	1 cup
1 tablespoon	brown sugar	1½ tablespoons
¾ teaspoon	salt	1 teaspoon
½ teaspoon	fennel seeds	¾ teaspoon
1 teaspoon	barley malt syrup*	1½ teaspoons
1 tablespoon	vegetable oil	1½ tablespoons
¾ cup plus 2 tablespoons	water	1¼ cups

Add all ingredients in the order suggested by your bread machine manual and process on the basic bread cycle according to the manufacturer's directions.

* Available in health food stores.

Five-Grain Sourdough Bread

This multi-grain bread features many textures—crunchy, soft, dense—and a lot of protein and fiber. I like it filled with sliced chicken and cucumber or tuna and tomato. It is best for breakfast untoasted and keeps for several days unrefrigerated if well wrapped.

SMALL LOAF (1 POUND)	INGREDIENTS	LARGE LOAF (1½ POUNDS)
1½ teaspoons	active dry yeast	2¼ teaspoons
1½ cups	bread flour	2¼ cups
¼ cup	amaranth flour *	¼ cup plus 2 tablespoons
¼ cup	whole wheat flour	¼ cup plus 2 tablespoons
¼ cup	soy flour	¼ cup plus 2 tablespoons
¼ cup	rolled oats	¼ cup plus 2 tablespoons
2 tablespoons	powdered milk	3 tablespoons
1 teaspoon	salt	1½ teaspoons
1 tablespoon	vegetable oil	1½ tablespoons
1 tablespoon	honey	1½ tablespoons
¼ cup	flax or sesame seeds	⅓ cup
¾ cup	sourdough starter (page 7) **	1 cup plus 2 tablespoons
½ cup	water	¾ cup

Add all ingredients in the order suggested by your bread machine manual and process on the basic bread cycle according to the manufacturer's directions. Let the loaf cool completely before slicing.

* Available in health food stores.

** After measuring out what is needed for this recipe, be sure to replenish your sourdough starter with equal amounts of flour and water.

Sunshine Bread

Everything you need for breakfast is in this crunchy, honey-and-orange–flavored bread. It stays moist for days and is so flavorful you need not use butter.

SMALL LOAF (1 POUND)	INGREDIENTS	LARGE LOAF (1½ POUNDS)
1½ teaspoons	active dry yeast	2¼ teaspoons
1½ cups	bread flour	2¼ cups
¼ cup	whole wheat flour	¼ cup plus 2 tablespoons
¼ cup	soy flour *	¼ cup plus 2 tablespoons
2 tablespoons	wheat germ	3 tablespoons
2 tablespoons	powdered milk	3 tablespoons
1 tablespoon	grated orange zest	1½ tablespoons
1 teaspoon	salt	1½ teaspoons
1 tablespoon	vegetable oil	1½ tablespoons
2 tablespoons	honey	3 tablespoons
¾ cup plus 2 tablespoons	water	1⅓ cups
¼ cup	shelled sunflower seeds	⅓ cup

1. Add all ingredients except the sunflower seeds in the order suggested by your bread machine manual and process on the basic bread cycle according to the manufacturer's directions.

2. At the beeper (or at the end of the first kneading in the Panasonic or National), add the sunflower seeds. Let the bread cool. Since this bread is dense, slice it thin.

* Available in health food stores.

Three-Grain Spa Bread

High in protein and low in salt, fat, and sugar, this bread still manages to be nutty and sweet. Since it is dense, cut into thin slices and serve for breakfast with cottage cheese or yogurt and fresh berries, as they do at the poshest spas. It is good warm or cooled and toasted.

SMALL LOAF (1 POUND)	INGREDIENTS	LARGE LOAF (1½ POUNDS)
1½ teaspoons	active dry yeast	2½ teaspoons
½ cup	bread flour	¾ cup
1¾ cups	whole wheat flour	2½ cups
¼ cup	rolled oats	⅓ cup
2 tablespoons	soy flour *	3 tablespoons
1 tablespoon	wheat germ	1½ tablespoons
½ teaspoon	salt	¾ teaspoon
3 tablespoons	powdered milk	¼ cup plus 1½ teaspoons
1 tablespoon	vegetable oil	1½ tablespoons
2 tablespoons	honey	3 tablespoons
¾ cup plus 2 tablespoons	water	1⅓ cups

Add all ingredients in the order suggested by your bread machine manual and process on the basic bread cycle according to the manufacturer's directions.

* Available in health food stores.

Trail Bread

Put this loaf in your backpack and travel: it is more filling than trail mix, not much heavier, and loaded with vitamins and energy-giving nutrients.

SMALL LOAF (1 POUND)	INGREDIENTS	LARGE LOAF (1½ POUNDS)
1½ teaspoons	active dry yeast	2¼ teaspoons
1 cup	bread flour	1½ cups
1 cup	whole wheat flour	1½ cups
¼ cup	rolled oats	¾ cup
1 teaspoon	salt	1½ teaspoons
1 tablespoon	vegetable oil	1½ tablespoons
2 tablespoons	honey	3 tablespoons
1 tablespoon	sesame seeds	1½ tablespoons
¾ cup plus 2 tablespoons	water	1¼ cups
¼ cup	trail mix: dried apple, chopped peanuts, shelled sunflower seeds, pumpkin or flax seeds, flaked coconut, raisins, and/or chocolate chips	¾ cup

1. Add all ingredients except the trail mix in the order suggested by your bread machine manual and process on the basic bread cycle according to the manufacturer's directions.

2. At the beeper (or at the end of the first kneading in the Panasonic or National), add any combination of trail mix ingredients.

High-Protein Bread

This is moist, dense, chewy bread that keeps well. Let it cool completely and slice thin for open-faced sandwiches with sliced tomatoes, cucumbers, or anything crunchy, even crumbled bacon.

SMALL LOAF (1 POUND)	INGREDIENTS	LARGE LOAF (1½ POUNDS)
¼ cup	quinoa grain	¼ cup plus 2 tablespoons
1 cup	milk	1½ cups
1½ teaspoons	active dry yeast	2½ teaspoons
1½ cups	bread flour	2¼ cups
¼ cup	amaranth flour	⅓ cup
¼ cup	soy flour*	⅓ cup
½ cup	wheat bran	¾ cup
1 teaspoon	salt	1½ teaspoons
2 tablespoons	honey	3 tablespoons
1 tablespoon	vegetable oil	1½ tablespoons
1 tablespoon	grated orange zest	1½ tablespoons

1. To cook quinoa, add it to twice its measure of boiling water. Simmer for 10 minutes. Drain off any excess liquid and let cool.

2. Scald the milk in a small saucepan and let cool to room temperature.

3. Add the cooked quinoa, milk, and remaining ingredients in the order suggested by your bread machine manual and process on the basic bread cycle according to the manufacturer's directions.

* Available in health food stores.

Seven Grains, Nuts, and Seeds Bread

Topped with cucumber and smoked trout, salmon, or anchovies, this dense, crunchy bread makes excellent canapés. It is firm enough to slice very thin, even when just cooled. Fill with radishes, sprouts, and tuna for a satisfying low-calorie sandwich.

SMALL LOAF (1 POUND)	INGREDIENTS	LARGE LOAF (1½ POUNDS)
1½ teaspoons	active dry yeast	2¼ teaspoons
1⅔ cups	bread flour	2½ cups
¾ cup	seven-grain cereal	1 cup plus 2 tablespoons
2 tablespoons	powdered milk	3 tablespoons
½ cup	chopped walnuts	¾ cup
½ teaspoon	salt	¾ teaspoon
1 tablespoon	vegetable oil	1½ tablespoons
2 tablespoons	unsulphured molasses	3 tablespoons
¾ cup plus 2 tablespoons	water	1¼ cups
¼ cup	seeds—any combination of sesame, shelled sunflower, flax, or pumpkin	⅓ cup

1. Add all ingredients except the seeds in the order suggested by your bread machine manual and process on the basic bread cycle according to the manufacturer's directions.

2. At the beeper (or at the end of the first kneading in the Panasonic or National), add the seeds.

Chapter Four

Holiday, Celebration, and Gift Breads

Here are breads for parties, for holidays, and special dinners, to give as gifts or to use for ceremony or celebration. Some are traditional, like Pandoro for Italian Christmas; others provide innovative party food such as Prosciutto and Black Pepper Bread. All are rich and festive enough to give as gifts for holidays or to say thank you. Thanks to the efficiency of the bread machine—which requires so little effort on the part of the baker—these breads, rich with butter, eggs, spices, and fruits, can be made at the busiest of holiday times.

Crisp, clear cellophane is the perfect wrapping for gift breads, because it lets the good looks of the loaf show through and has a snappier, more festive look than plastic wrap. It can be found in specialty paper and party shops. Place a completely cooled bread in the center of a large square of cellophane. (If the bread is still warm, it will get soggy inside the wrapping.) Gather up the edges in one hand and tie with a colorful ribbon. If you want to bring a bread still warm as a gift, wrap it in a new cloth napkin or kitchen towel or place in a basket lined with cloth or good-quality paper napkins.

Baba au Rhum

Save this giant baba for a special celebration that calls for an impressive dessert that is syrupy and rich. It is especially nice on cold nights with hot coffee or cappuccino.

SMALL LOAF (1 POUND)	INGREDIENTS	LARGE LOAF (1½ POUNDS)
BABA		
¼ cup	milk	⅓ cup
1¼ teaspoons	active dry yeast	1½ teaspoons
1¼ cups plus 2 tablespoons	bread flour	1¾ cups plus 2 tablespoons
5 tablespoons	sugar	6 tablespoons
5 tablespoons	unsalted butter	8 tablespoons (1 stick)
2	eggs	3
SYRUP		
1 cup	sugar	
1 cup	water	
¼ cup	dark rum	
⅔ cup	unsweetened whipped cream	1 cup

1. Scald the milk in a small saucepan and let cool to room temperature.

2. Add the milk and all remaining ingredients for the baba in the order suggested by your bread machine manual and process on the basic bread cycle according to the manufacturer's directions.

3. Make a syrup by boiling the sugar and water together in a small saucepan until the mixture is clear. Add the rum and simmer for 1 minute.

4. When the bread cycle ends, remove the warm baba to a deep dish or shallow bowl. Brush the baba with the syrup several times as it cools. Allow the baba to soak up the syrup that collects in the bottom of the dish. Refrigerate until chilled.

5. When cool, slice the baba into wedges and brush them with any remaining syrup if they are not totally moist. Serve with unsweetened whipped cream on the side.

Black Forest–Chocolate Cherry Bread

This bread is even better—and more like its namesake cake—when topped with a dollop of whipped cream.

SMALL LOAF (1 POUND)	INGREDIENTS	LARGE LOAF (1½ POUNDS)
⅔ cup	water	1 cup
⅓ cup	unsweetened cocoa powder	½ cup
1½ teaspoons	active dry yeast	2½ teaspoons
1¾ cups plus 2 tablespoons	bread flour	2¾ cups
⅓ cup	sugar	½ cup
1 teaspoon	salt	1½ teaspoons
2 tablespoons	unsalted butter	3 tablespoons
1 yolk	egg	1 whole
½ cup	dried tart cherries	¾ cup
¼ cup	kirsch or rum (optional)	¼ cup plus 2 tablespoons

1. Bring the water to a boil in a small saucepan. Add the cocoa powder and stir until completely dissolved. Let cool to room temperature.

2. Add the cocoa and all remaining ingredients except the cherries and the kirsch or rum in the order suggested by your bread machine manual and process on the basic bread cycle according to the manufacturer's directions.

3. Meanwhile, soak the cherries in half of the kirsch or rum. At the beeper (or at the end of the first kneading in the Panasonic or National), add the cherries and their soaking liquid.

4. When you remove the bread from the machine, brush the remaining kirsch or rum over the top of the loaf. Serve warm or cooled.

Butterscotch Whole Wheat Bread

Finding ribbons of caramelized brown sugar laced inside a whole wheat bread is a sweet surprise and a good enticement for young people who think they do not like whole wheat bread. This moist loaf is best as a snack or dessert, especially with pears.

SMALL LOAF (1 POUND)	INGREDIENTS	LARGE LOAF (1½ POUNDS)
2 tablespoons	butter	3 tablespoons
½ cup	brown sugar	¾ cup
1½ teaspoons	active dry yeast	2¼ teaspoons
1¼ cups	bread flour	1¾ cups plus 2 tablespoons
1 cup	whole wheat flour	1½ cups
2 tablespoons	powdered milk	3 tablespoons
½ teaspoon	salt	¾ teaspoon
2 tablespoons	sugar	3 tablespoons
1	egg	1
2 tablespoons	vegetable oil	3 tablespoons
⅔ cup	water	1 cup

1. Cook the butter and brown sugar together over medium-low heat until the sugar bubbles and melts. Let cool.

2. Add the brown sugar mixture and all remaining ingredients in the order suggested by your bread machine manual and process on the basic bread cycle according to the manufacturer's directions.

Chelsea Bread

For several hundred years the English have served Chelsea buns for tea. After currants and lemon peel were sprinkled on plain dough, it was rolled up, sliced, and the pieces placed side by side to rise. They were baked and then torn into buns.

This bread is a loaf version, and it disappears too fast. It is best served warm, when very soft and sweet. For brunch or tea, it stands on its own, with no need for butter or jam, and it is a first-rate coffee cake.

SMALL LOAF (1 POUND)	INGREDIENTS	LARGE LOAF (1½ POUNDS)
1 tablespoon	candied lemon zest (page 136)	1½ tablespoons
1 teaspoon	active dry yeast	1½ teaspoons
2 cups	bread flour	3 cups
2 tablespoons	powdered milk	3 tablespoons
3 tablespoons	sugar	¼ cup
½ teaspoon	salt	¾ teaspoon
4 tablespoons	unsalted butter	6 tablespoons
⅔ cup	water	1 cup
½ cup	currants	¾ cup
½ cup	confectioners' sugar	
2 tablespoons	reserved syrup from candied lemon peel	

1. Add all ingredients except the currants, confectioners' sugar, and lemon syrup in the order suggested by your bread machine manual and process on the basic bread cycle according to the manufacturer's directions.

2. At the beeper (or at the end of the first kneading in the Panasonic or National), add the currants.

3. After the bread is removed from the machine, let cool slightly. Make a glaze by blending the confectioners' sugar with the lemon syrup. Pour over the barely warm bread.

Cherries and Ricotta Cheese Bread

Just a little sweet and studded with tart cherries, this lush bread is delightful warm, spread with butter for a snack or dessert with coffee or hot chocolate. If there are leftovers, turn them into outstanding cinnamon toast: Butter bread slices, sprinkle generously with cinnamon and sugar, and broil briefly until the sugar caramelizes.

SMALL LOAF (1 POUND)	INGREDIENTS	LARGE LOAF (1½ POUNDS)
1½ teaspoons	active dry yeast	2¼ teaspoons
1¼ cups	bread flour	1¾ cups plus 2 tablespoons
1 cup	whole wheat flour	1½ cups
2 tablespoons	sugar	3 tablespoons
1 teaspoon	salt	1½ teaspoons
½ teaspoon	ground cinnamon	¾ teaspoon
2	eggs	3
½ cup	ricotta cheese	¾ cup
4 tablespoons	unsalted butter	6 tablespoons
¼ cup	water	⅓ cup
½ cup	dried cherries	⅔ cup

1. Add all ingredients except the cherries according to your bread machine manual and process on the basic bread cycle according to the manufacturer's directions.

2. At the beeper (or at the end of the first kneading in the Panasonic or National), add the dried cherries.

Sweet and Zesty Cornbread

Serve this cakelike bread after a Mexican meal, with melon or berries for dessert, or offer it for tea. Strong coffee and this lively bread also make a pleasant way to wake up in the morning.

SMALL LOAF (1 POUND)	INGREDIENTS	LARGE LOAF (1½ POUNDS)
1½ teaspoons	active dry yeast	2½ teaspoons
1¼ cups	bread flour	1¾ cups plus 2 tablespoons
1 cup	yellow cornmeal	1½ cups
2 tablespoons	powdered milk	3 tablespoons
⅓ cup	sugar	½ cup
½ teaspoon	salt	¾ teaspoon
1	egg(s)	2
2 tablespoons	grated orange zest	3 tablespoons
2 tablespoons	unsalted butter	3 tablespoons
¼ teaspoon	ground black pepper	½ teaspoon
¾ cup	water	1 cup
½ cup	currants	¾ cup

1. Add all ingredients except the currants in the order suggested by your bread machine manual and process on the basic bread cycle according to the manufacturer's directions.

2. At the beeper (or at the end of the first kneading in the Panasonic or National), add the currants.

Cranberry Orange Bread

This bread can easily become a Thanksgiving tradition. You need something to sustain you all morning while you smell the turkey cooking. Leftovers make a fine school lunch along with a drumstick or chicken wings.

SMALL LOAF (1 POUND)	INGREDIENTS	LARGE LOAF (1½ POUNDS)
⅓ cup	fresh cranberries	½ cup
1½ teaspoons	active dry yeast	2¼ teaspoons
2 cups	bread flour	3 cups
¼ cup	rolled oats	⅓ cup
3 tablespoons	cracked wheat	¼ cup
3 tablespoons	sugar	¼ cup
½ teaspoon	salt	¾ teaspoon
1 tablespoon	grated orange zest	1½ tablespoons
3 tablespoons	vegetable oil	¼ cup
1	whole egg	1
0	egg yolks	1
⅓ cup	orange juice	½ cup
⅓ cup	water	½ cup

1. Coarsely chop the cranberries. Freeze until hard.

2. Add all remaining ingredients except the cranberries in the order suggested by your bread machine manual and process on the basic bread cycle according to the manufacturer's directions.

3. At the beeper (or at the end of the first kneading in the Panasonic or National), add the frozen chopped cranberries.

Date Nut Bread

Moist, sweet, healthful, and long lasting, this loaf tastes of fruit and cinnamon, with a crunch of nuts. Make it into the classic tea sandwich with cream cheese or spread with ricotta cheese and grill until golden. But give me mine straight; a bread this full of goodness doesn't need any new-fangled jimcrackies. It makes a wonderful gift, too.

SMALL LOAF (1 POUND)	INGREDIENTS	LARGE LOAF (1½ POUNDS)
1½ teaspoons	active dry yeast	2¼ teaspoons
1½ cups	bread flour	2¼ cups
½ cup	wheat bran	¾ cup
½ cup	brown sugar	¾ cup
¾ teaspoon	salt	1¼ teaspoons
¾ teaspoon	ground cinnamon	1 teaspoon
2 tablespoons	butter	3 tablespoons
1	egg	1
¾ cup	water	1¼ cups
⅔ cup	chopped pitted dates	1 cup
½ cup	chopped walnuts	¾ cup

1. Add all ingredients except the dates and walnuts in the order suggested by your bread machine manual and process on the basic bread cycle according to the manufacturer's directions.

2. At the beeper (or at the end of the first kneading in the Panasonic or National), add the dates and walnuts. Let the bread cool before slicing.

Rich Fig Bread

This is just sweet enough for a peanut butter sandwich, but you won't need the jelly. Or serve plain or toasted with scrambled eggs.

SMALL LOAF (1 POUND)	INGREDIENTS	LARGE LOAF (1½ POUNDS)
1½ teaspoons	active dry yeast	2¼ teaspoons
2 cups	bread flour	3 cups
2 tablespoons	wheat germ	3 tablespoons
3 tablespoons	sugar	¼ cup
½ teaspoon	salt	1 teaspoon
¼ teaspoon	ground cloves	½ teaspoon
2 tablespoons	unsalted butter	3 tablespoons
1	egg	1
½ cup	chopped dried figs	⅔ cup
½ cup	water	¾ cup plus 2 tablespoons

Add all ingredients in the order suggested by your bread machine manual and process on the basic bread cycle according to the manufacturer's directions.

Gingerbread

Here is all the wonderful spicy flavor of the usual ginger quick bread incorporated in the tear-apart texture of a yeast bread. The smells of ginger and rye baking are divine. Serve slightly warm with vanilla ice cream or whipped cream. When it cools, make tea sandwiches filled with cream cheese.

SMALL LOAF (1 POUND)	INGREDIENTS	LARGE LOAF (1½ POUNDS)
¾ cup plus 2 tablespoons	milk	1¼ cups
2 tablespoons	unsalted butter	3 tablespoons
¼ cup	brown sugar	6 tablespoons
1½ teaspoons	active dry yeast	2¼ teaspoons
1¾ cups	bread flour	2⅔ cups
½ cup	rye flour	¾ cup
1 teaspoon	salt	1½ teaspoons
1½ teaspoons	ground ginger	2 teaspoons
½ teaspoon	ground cinnamon	¾ teaspoon
¼ teaspoon	grated nutmeg	¼ teaspoon
Pinch	ground cloves	¼ teaspoon

1. Scald the milk. Stir in the butter and brown sugar. Let cool to room temperature.
2. Add the milk mixture and all remaining ingredients in the order suggested by your bread machine manual and process on the basic bread cycle according to the manufacturer's directions.

Hawaiian Pineapple and Macadamia Loaf

On its own, this bread is a great snack with cold milk, tea, or coffee. It makes an exotic sandwich with chicken salad or honey-cured ham.

SMALL LOAF (1 POUND)	INGREDIENTS	LARGE LOAF (1½ POUNDS)
1¼ teaspoons	active dry yeast	2 teaspoons
1¾ cups plus 2 tablespoons	bread flour	2¾ cups plus 1 tablespoon
½ cup	cracked wheat	¾ cup
2 tablespoons	yellow cornmeal	3 tablespoons
2 tablespoons	brown sugar	3 tablespoons
2 tablespoons	powdered milk	3 tablespoons
½ teaspoon	ground ginger	¾ teaspoon
1 teaspoon	salt	1½ teaspoons
1 tablespoon	vegetable oil	1½ tablespoons
½ cup	flaked coconut	¾ cup
½ cup	canned pineapple chunks	¾ cup
¼ cup	pineapple juice reserved from canned pineapple	⅓ cup
⅓ cup	water	½ cup
¼ cup	chopped macadamia nuts	⅓ cup

1. Add all ingredients except the nuts in the order suggested by your bread machine manual and process on the basic bread cycle according to the manufacturer's directions.
2. At the beeper (or at the end of the first kneading in the Panasonic or National), add the nuts.

Figgy Rye Bread

If you eat slices of warm figgy rye smeared lightly with butter, you will forget about those childish fig cookies. It makes a yummy sandwich with cream cheese. Or toast and top with ricotta or cottage cheese or a thin slice of prosciutto.

SMALL LOAF (1 POUND)	INGREDIENTS	LARGE LOAF (1½ POUNDS)
1¼ teaspoons	active dry yeast	2 teaspoons
1½ cups	bread flour	2¼ cups
¾ cup	rye flour	1 cup plus 2 tablespoons
2 tablespoons	powdered milk	3 tablespoons
1 tablespoon	brown sugar	1½ tablespoons
1 teaspoon	salt	1½ teaspoons
¼ teaspoon	ground ginger	½ teaspoon
¼ teaspoon	ground cinnamon	½ teaspoon
1 teaspoon	barley malt syrup*	1½ teaspoons
2 tablespoons	unsalted butter	3 tablespoons
¾ cup plus 2 tablespoons	water	1¼ cups
½ cup	chopped dry figs	⅔ cup

1. Add all ingredients except the figs in the order suggested by your bread machine manual and process on the basic bread cycle according to the manufacturer's directions.

2. At the beeper (or at the end of the first kneading in the Panasonic or National), add the figs.

* Available in health food stores.

Cheese Brioche

Believe it or not, the bread machine version of cheese brioche is better than any I have ever made by hand. This recipe is adapted from a brioche in Bernard Clayton's 1977 Breads of France, *which required four kneadings and ten hours of rising. Cheese brioche is super rich, very light, and just cheesy enough. There is no need to spread with butter; it's in the bread. Serve with an omelet, a salad, or just a bunch of grapes.*

SMALL LOAF (1 POUND)	INGREDIENTS	LARGE LOAF (1½ POUNDS)
1½ teaspoons	active dry yeast	2¼ teaspoons
1¾ cups	bread flour	2⅔ cups
1½ teaspoons	sugar	2¼ teaspoons
1 teaspoon	salt	1½ teaspoons
6 tablespoons	unsalted butter	8 tablespoons
2	eggs	3
½ cup	water	¾ cup
⅓ cup	finely diced Swiss cheese	½ cup

1. Add all ingredients except the Swiss cheese in the order suggested by your bread machine manual and process on the basic bread cycle according to the manufacturer's directions.

2. At the beeper (or at the end of the first kneading in the Panasonic or National), add the Swiss cheese.

Peanut Butter Chocolate Chip Bread

This one is really for the kids, although I know kids with beards that love it. Only a glass of cold milk will do it justice. With the chocolate glaze plus colored sprinkles and a candle, it can even be turned into a birthday cake.

SMALL LOAF (1 POUND)	INGREDIENTS	LARGE LOAF (1½ POUNDS)
1 cup	chocolate chips	1½ cups
1½ teaspoons	active dry yeast	2¼ teaspoons
2 cups	bread flour	3 cups
2 tablespoons	wheat germ	3 tablespoons
2 tablespoons	powdered milk	3 tablespoons
3 tablespoons	brown sugar	¼ cup
1 teaspoon	salt	1½ teaspoons
⅓ cup	peanut butter	½ cup
¾ cup plus 2 tablespoons	water	1¼ cups

1. Freeze the chocolate chips.

2. Add all ingredients except the chocolate chips in the order suggested by your bread machine manual and process on the basic bread cycle according to the manufacturer's directions.

3. At the beeper (or at the end of the first kneading in the Panasonic or National), add half of the chocolate chips.

4. When the bread cycle ends, remove the bread from the machine and let cool for ½ hour. Melt the remaining half of the chocolate chips in a double boiler over barely simmering water or in a microwave oven. Pour the melted chocolate over the bread and let it dribble down the sides.

Pandoro de Verona

This recipe is inspired by Carol Field's The Italian Baker, *probably my favorite baking book. In Italy, bread comes from the village bakery; no one bakes bread at home, especially very difficult bread like pandoro. With a bread machine, this bread is not only possible, it is easy and outstanding. If you like panettone, you will love this lighter, more delicate Christmas bread from the north of Italy. Give pandoro as a Christmas or New Year's gift.*

SMALL LOAF (1 POUND)	INGREDIENTS	LARGE LOAF (1½ POUNDS)
FIRST DOUGH		
1 teaspoon	active dry yeast	1¾ teaspoons
¾ cup	bread flour	1 cup plus 2 tablespoons
2 tablespoons	sugar	3 tablespoons
1 tablespoon	unsalted butter	3 tablespoons
1	whole egg	1
0	egg yolk	1
2 tablespoons	water	3 tablespoons
SECOND DOUGH		
1 cup	bread flour	1¼ cups
¼ cup	sugar	⅓ cup
¼ teaspoon	salt	½ teaspoon
1	whole egg	2
1	egg yolk	0

½ teaspoon	vanilla extract	1 teaspoon
3 tablespoons	unsalted butter	5 tablespoons
2 tablespoons	candied orange zest (page 136)	3 tablespoons
2 tablespoons	candied lemon zest (page 136)	3 tablespoons

1. Add all ingredients for the first dough in the order suggested by your bread machine manual and process on the basic bread cycle according to the manufacturer's directions.

2. At the beeper (or at the end of the first kneading in the Panasonic or National), turn off the machine but leave the first dough in the machine.

3. Add all ingredients for the second dough in the order suggested by your bread machine manual and process both doughs together on the basic bread cycle according to the manufacturer's directions.

4. Let the loaf cool completely in the bread pan—at least 2 hours—so that the sides will be crisp and strong enough to support the top.

Panettone

This Christmas bread from Milan is now available around the world, packed in domed boxes by huge Italian bakeries. The panettone from your own bread machine, though, will be softer, fruitier, and more buttery. Cut into wedges or thick slices for Christmas morning, or slice thinner for a New Year's Day dessert buffet. Panettone can be turned into fine French toast that is sweet enough to forgo maple syrup.

SMALL LOAF (1 POUND)	INGREDIENTS	LARGE LOAF (1½ POUNDS)
1¼ teaspoons	active dry yeast	2 teaspoons
1¾ cups plus 2 tablespoons	bread flour	2¾ cups plus 2 tablespoons
¾ teaspoon	salt	1 teaspoon
2½ tablespoons	candied orange or lemon zest (page 136)	¼ cup
2½ tablespoons	sugar	¼ cup
2½ tablespoons	butter	4 tablespoons (½ stick)
1	whole egg(s)	2
2	egg yolks	2
⅓ cup	water	½ cup
⅓ cup	raisins	½ cup

1. Add all ingredients except the raisins in the order suggested by your bread machine manual and process on the basic bread cycle according to the manufacturer's directions.

2. At the beeper (or at the end of the first kneading in the Panasonic or National), add the raisins.

Prosciutto and Black Pepper Bread

Serve this tasty bread with an antipasto or alone as an hors d'oeuvre. It makes a meal with a bowl of soup, such as minestrone, chicken with escarole, or French onion. Salty ham, such as Smithfield, can be substituted for the prosciutto.

SMALL LOAF (1 POUND)	INGREDIENTS	LARGE LOAF (1½ POUNDS)
1½ teaspoons	active dry yeast	2¼ teaspoons
2 cups	bread flour	3 cups
1½ teaspoons	sugar	1 tablespoon
1 teaspoon	salt	1½ teaspoons
½ teaspoon	ground black pepper	¾ teaspoon
½ cup	chopped prosciutto including the fat	¾ cup
¼ cup	olive oil	⅓ cup
¾ cup	water	1 cup plus 2 tablespoons

Add all ingredients in the order suggested by your bread machine manual and process on the basic bread cycle according to the manufacturer's directions.

Prune and Almond Bread

This is a little less sweet than date nut bread, but very moist and rich. It is fine on its own for a snack or with cream cheese or butter or thinly sliced apple. It keeps and travels well, especially on ski trips.

SMALL LOAF (1 POUND)	INGREDIENTS	LARGE LOAF (1½ POUNDS)
¾ cup	milk	1 cup plus 2 tablespoons
2 tablespoons	unsalted butter	3 tablespoons
¼ cup	honey	⅓ cup
1½ teaspoons	active dry yeast	2¼ teaspoons
1¼ cups	bread flour	2 cups
1 cup	whole wheat flour	1½ cups
¾ teaspoon	salt	1 teaspoon
⅛ teaspoon	ground cloves	¼ teaspoon
½ cup	chopped pitted prunes	¾ cup
1	egg	1
1 teaspoon	caramel coloring* (optional)	1½ teaspoons
¼ cup	sliced or chopped almonds	⅓ cup

1. Scald the milk. Stir in the butter and honey. Let the mixture cool to room temperature.

2. Add the milk mixture and all remaining ingredients except the almonds according to your bread machine manual and process on the basic bread cycle according to the manufacturer's directions.

3. At the beeper (or at the end of the first kneading in the Panasonic or National), add the almonds. Let the bread cool before slicing.

* Mail-order source on page 11.

Ricotta and Fennel Sweet Bread

As sophisticated as this bread sounds, it is, nevertheless, the favorite of the feistiest ten-year-old Little Leaguer I know. It is light, sweet, spicy, and lovely for dessert with grapes or berries, poached pears, or baked apples.

SMALL LOAF (1 POUND)	INGREDIENTS	LARGE LOAF (1½ POUNDS)
1½ teaspoons	active dry yeast	2¼ teaspoons
2 cups	bread flour	3 cups
1 teaspoon	salt	1½ teaspoons
1 tablespoon	anise or fennel seeds	1½ tablespoons
¼ teaspoon	ground cinnamon	½ teaspoon
2 tablespoons	honey	3 tablespoons
1	egg(s)	2
¼ cup	ricotta cheese	⅓ cup
8 tablespoons	unsalted butter	12 tablespoons
3 tablespoons	water	¼ cup

Add all ingredients in the order suggested by your bread machine manual and process on the basic bread cycle according to the manufacturer's directions.

Double Pumpkin Bread

You could make this from your old jack-o-lantern, but it is much easier with canned pumpkin and already shelled seeds. Spread the slices with cream cheese, cottage cheese, or butter.

SMALL LOAF (1 POUND)	INGREDIENTS	LARGE LOAF (1½ POUNDS)
1½ teaspoons	active dry yeast	2¼ teaspoons
1 cup plus 2 tablespoons	bread flour	1⅔ cups
1 cup	whole wheat flour	1½ cups
2 tablespoons	powdered milk	3 tablespoons
2 tablespoons	brown sugar	3 tablespoons
1 teaspoon	ground ginger	1½ teaspoons
1 teaspoon	grated nutmeg	1½ teaspoons
1 teaspoon	ground cinnamon	1½ teaspoons
1 teaspoon	salt	1½ teaspoons
1 tablespoon	vegetable oil	1½ tablespoons
½ cup	canned pumpkin	¾ cup
½ cup plus 2 tablespoons	water	¾ cup plus 3 tablespoons
½ cup	shelled pumpkin seeds	¾ cup

1. Add all ingredients except the pumpkin seeds in the order suggested by your bread machine manual and process on the basic bread cycle according to the manufacturer's directions.

2. At the beeper (or at the end of the first kneading in the Panasonic or National), add the pumpkin seeds.

Sweet Potato and Pecan Bread

There is no need to wait until Thanksgiving to eat sweet potatoes. They are available year round, and this caramel-flavored bread tastes wonderful in any season with yogurt and fruit on the side or spread with cream cheese. For the child in all of us, top a slice with a few mini marshmallows and broil until golden.

SMALL LOAF (1 POUND)	INGREDIENTS	LARGE LOAF (1½ POUNDS)
1½ teaspoons	active dry yeast	2¼ teaspoons
1½ cups	bread flour	2¼ cups
½ cup	whole wheat flour	¾ cup
2 tablespoons	powdered milk	3 tablespoons
3 tablespoons	brown sugar	¼ cup
1 teaspoon	salt	1½ teaspoons
1 tablespoon	grated orange zest	1½ tablespoons
3 tablespoons	unsalted butter	4 tablespoons
¾ cup	mashed cooked sweet potato	1 cup
½ cup	water	¾ cup
¼ cup	coarsely chopped pecans	⅓ cup

1. Add all ingredients except the chopped pecans in the order suggested by your bread machine manual and process on the basic bread cycle according to the manufacturer's directions.

2. At the beeper (or at the end of the first kneading in the Panasonic or National), add the pecans.

Christmas Stollen

In Germany, dense, fruited stollen is a Christmas tradition. The machine version will not be as high as the traditional bread, but it will taste like a holiday treat. Unsliced, stollen lasts several days, on hand for holiday entertaining and gift giving.

SMALL LOAF (1 POUND)	INGREDIENTS	LARGE LOAF (1½ POUNDS)
DOUGH		
1¾ teaspoons	active dry yeast	2½ teaspoons
2 cups	bread flour	3 cups
3 tablespoons	sugar	¼ cup
¾ teaspoon	salt	1 teaspoon
2 tablespoons	powdered milk	3 tablespoons
4 tablespoons	unsalted butter	6 tablespoons
½ teaspoon	vanilla extract	¾ teaspoon
3 tablespoons	candied orange zest (page 136)	¼ cup
3 tablespoons	candied lemon zest (page 136)	¼ cup
¼ cup	dried tart cherries	⅓ cup
¼ cup	golden raisins	⅓ cup
1	egg	1
½ cup	water	¾ cup
2 tablespoons	chopped almonds	3 tablespoons

| ⅓ cup | confectioners' sugar | ½ cup |
| 1 tablespoon | lemon juice or water | 1½ tablespoons |

1. Add all ingredients for the dough except the chopped almonds in the order suggested by your bread machine manual and process on the basic bread cycle according to the manufacturer's directions.

2. At the beeper (or at the end of the first kneading in the Panasonic or National), add the almonds.

3. Remove the baked stollen from the machine. To make the glaze, mix the confectioners' sugar and juice or water until smooth. Pour over the warm stollen.

Tutti Dried Frutti Bread

For breakfast, ricotta or cottage cheese is fine on top of slices of this loaf; for lunch spread cream cheese between the slices. Toasted, this spiced fruited bread is sweet enough to satisfy late-night cravings.

SMALL LOAF (1 POUND)	INGREDIENTS	LARGE LOAF (1½ POUNDS)
1½ teaspoons	active dry yeast	2½ teaspoons
1½ cups	bread flour	2¼ cups
¾ cup	whole wheat flour	1 cup plus 2 tablespoons
2 tablespoons	rolled oats	3 tablespoons
1 teaspoon	salt	1½ teaspoons
2 tablespoons	unsalted butter	3 tablespoons
2 tablespoons	honey	3 tablespoons
¼ teaspoon	ground cloves	½ teaspoon
¼ cup	chopped pitted prunes	⅓ cup
¾ cup	water	1 cup plus 2 tablespoons
1 cup	*dried* fruit (any combination of dried figs, apricots, raisins, currants, cherries, apples, and/or pears)	1½ cups

1. Add all ingredients except the mixed dried fruit in the order suggested by your bread machine manual and process on the basic bread cycle according to the manufacturer's directions.

2. At the beeper (or at the end of the first kneading in the Panasonic or National), gradually add the mixed dried fruit.

Very Orange Tea Bread

Tart and sweet, perfumed with fresh orange, this loaf is more cake than bread. It needs no filling or topping; it is satisfying as is with hot or iced tea or with Champagne. I like to bring it as a house gift. It will last several days well wrapped.

SMALL LOAF (1 POUND)	INGREDIENTS	LARGE LOAF (1½ POUNDS)
½ cup	milk	¾ cup
1½ tablespoons	candied orange zest (recipe follows)	2½ tablespoons
3 tablespoons	syrup from candied orange zest	¼ cup
1½ teaspoons	active dry yeast	2¼ teaspoons
2 cups	bread flour	3 cups
3 tablespoons	wheat bran	¼ cup
¾ teaspoon	salt	1¼ teaspoons
2 tablespoons	unsalted butter	3 tablespoons
1	egg	1

1. Scald the milk. Let cool to room temperature.

2. Add the cooled milk and all remaining ingredients in the order suggested by your bread machine manual and process on the basic bread cycle according to the manufacturer's directions.

Candied Orange Zest

For each tablespoon of chopped zest required for a recipe, use 1 medium orange. With a swivel-bladed vegetable peeler, remove all the orange-colored skin, or zest, from the orange, leaving behind the bitter white pith underneath. Finely chop or dice the zest.

In a small saucepan, combine ⅓ cup water and ⅓ cup sugar. Bring to a boil over medium heat, swirling the pan until the sugar dissolves and the liquid is clear. (For 2 oranges use ⅔ cup each water and sugar; for 3 oranges, 1 cup, etc.)

Add the zest and boil for 5 minutes. Let the candied zest cool in the syrup and refrigerate it in a covered jar in the syrup for up to 3 weeks. Before using, drain the zest, reserving the syrup, which is called for in some recipes and is delicious over fruit and ice cream.

Candied Lemon Zest

Substitute the zest of a large lemon for the orange and proceed as directed above.

Chapter Five

Breads with an International Flavor

From France and Italy, Kenya and China come recipes and flavors made into breads that are both traditional and unique. With the electric bread machine, even the busiest baker can whip up an impressive, exotic loaf on a moment's notice. Even brioche, the most difficult of all breads, is not a problem. Instead of messing with this very sticky dough by hand or in a food processor, your bread machine will turn out the lightest, richest brioche imaginable. As a professional baker with high standards to uphold, I was truly impressed with the fine quality of this delectable bread.

In the bread machine, flour, yeast, and spices come together in a worldly loaf, classic in texture, but often unique in flavor. The renowned taste of béarnaise sauce, for example, can be translated into bread, thus doing away with the fat of the sauce but none of its flavor. Other breads that follow are full of surprises, too—whole hard-cooked eggs, spices, sausages. Consider slicing and serving these loaves as hors d'oeuvres for a crowd. The variety in this chapter alone can keep guests tasting into the night.

Alsatian Hazelnut Whole Wheat Bread

Any hearty soup, especially French onion or cream of mushroom, tastes good with this substantial bread. It is crusty, can be sliced thick or thin, and toasts well. For breakfast or with tea, spread with pear or apple butter or apricot jam.

SMALL LOAF (1 POUND)	INGREDIENTS	LARGE LOAF (1½ POUNDS)
⅔ cup	milk	1 cup
1½ teaspoons	active dry yeast	2¼ teaspoons
⅔ cup	bread flour	1 cup
1¼ cups	whole wheat flour	2¼ cups
2 tablespoons	brown sugar	3 tablespoons
½ teaspoon	salt	¾ teaspoon
2 tablespoons	chopped toasted hazelnuts	3 tablespoons
1 tablespoon	vegetable oil	1½ tablespoons
1	whole egg	1
0	egg yolk	1
¼ cup	raisins or currants	⅓ cup

1. Scald the milk. Let cool to room temperature.

2. Add the milk and all remaining ingredients except the raisins in the order suggested by your bread machine manual and process on the basic bread cycle according to the manufacturer's directions.

3. At the beeper (or at the end of the first kneading in the Panasonic or National), add the raisins or currants.

Béarnaise Bread

Filled with sliced fillet of beef, this bread makes the ultimate steak sandwich. The loaf is dense and intensely flavored, so slice it thinly enough to let the taste of the meat come through. Scented with tarragon, this bread is also good with an omelet or cold roast chicken.

SMALL LOAF (1 POUND)	INGREDIENTS	LARGE LOAF (1½ POUNDS)
1½ teaspoons	active dry yeast	2¼ teaspoons
1½ cups plus 2 tablespoons	bread flour	2¼ cups plus 1 tablespoon
½ cup	whole wheat flour	¾ cup
2 tablespoons	wheat germ	3 tablespoons
1 tablespoon	sugar	1½ tablespoons
1 teaspoon	salt	1½ teaspoons
1 tablespoon	dried tarragon	1½ tablespoons
1½ teaspoons	sharp Dijon mustard	2¼ teaspoons
¼ teaspoon	ground black pepper	¼ teaspoon
2 tablespoons	vegetable oil	3 tablespoons
1	egg	1
¼ cup	tarragon vinegar	¼ cup plus 2 tablespoons
⅔ cup	water	1 cup

Add all ingredients in the order suggested by your bread machine manual and process on the basic bread cycle according to the manufacturer's directions. Let the loaf cool before slicing.

Brioche Loaf

This is the richest dough, the ultimate French breakfast bread, just light and sweet enough to eat with eggs, pâté, or ham. Slice thick to toast or to make into moist, elegant French toast. Since this recipe contains such a high proportion of butter, it must be added gradually so that it will be absorbed. This will only add about ten minutes to the time you spend at the machine.

SMALL LOAF (1 POUND)	INGREDIENTS	LARGE LOAF (1½ POUNDS)
1¼ teaspoons	active dry yeast	1¾ teaspoons
1¼ cups	bread flour	1¾ cups plus 2 tablespoons
2 tablespoons	sugar	3 tablespoons
½ teaspoon	salt	¾ teaspoon
1	whole egg(s)	2
1	egg yolk	1
¼ cup	water	¼ cup plus 2 tablespoons
6 tablespoons	unsalted butter	8 tablespoons

1. Add all ingredients except the butter in the order suggested by your bread machine manual and process on the basic bread cycle according to the manufacturer's directions.

2. Cut the butter into tablespoon-size pieces. About 10 minutes before the end of your first kneading cycle, begin adding the butter, 1 tablespoon each minute. Do not rush it. Let the machine continue its process.

3. At the end of the entire cycle, let the brioche cool in the opened machine about 20 minutes. This will keep the sides firm while the center stays moist.

Eastern European Crackling Bread

Every cuisine has its form of cracklings. The Chinese and the French treasure crisp duck skin; Eastern Europeans render the fat from bits of chicken skin, leaving crispy bits of skin to sprinkle on mashed potatoes.

SMALL LOAF (1 POUND)	INGREDIENTS	LARGE LOAF (1½ POUNDS)
1	skin of a 3- to 4-pound chicken or duck	1
1	garlic clove(s), minced	2
1¼ teaspoons	active dry yeast	2 teaspoons
2 cups	bread flour	3 cups
¼ cup	cracked wheat	⅓ cup
1 tablespoon	sugar	1½ tablespoons
½ teaspoon	dried rosemary	1 teaspoon
1 teaspoon	salt	1½ teaspoons
¼ teaspoon	ground black pepper	½ teaspoon
1 tablespoon	vinegar	1½ tablespoons
¾ cup plus 2 tablespoons	water	1¼ cups

1. Cut the chicken or duck skin into ½-inch pieces. In a large nonstick skillet, cook the skin over low heat, stirring occasionally, until the fat is rendered and the skin is golden, about 20 minutes. Add the garlic and cook until the skin is crisp, 5 to 10 minutes longer. Drain off all but 1 tablespoon fat.

2. Add the crisp skin with the reserved fat and all remaining ingredients in the order suggested by your bread machine manual and process on the basic bread cycle according to the manufacturer's directions.

Curried Pumpkin and Banana Bread

This bread is spicy, sweet, and fruity at the same time—too assertive for any filling except cream cheese or unsalted butter. A few slices and an apple, pear, or glass of milk make a satisfying snack.

SMALL LOAF (1 POUND)	INGREDIENTS	LARGE LOAF (1½ POUNDS)
1½ teaspoons	active dry yeast	2¼ teaspoons
1 cup plus 2 tablespoons	bread flour	1¾ cups
1 cup	whole wheat flour	1½ cups
2 tablespoons	cracked wheat	3 tablespoons
1 teaspoon	curry powder	1½ teaspoons
½ teaspoon	minced garlic	1 teaspoon
1 tablespoon	sesame seeds	1½ tablespoons
2 tablespoons	sugar	3 tablespoons
½ cup	mashed ripe banana	¾ cup
½ cup	canned pumpkin	¾ cup
1 tablespoon	vegetable oil	1½ tablespoons
¼ cup	water	⅓ cup

Add all ingredients in the order suggested by your bread machine manual and process on the basic bread cycle according to the manufacturer's directions. Let the loaf cool before slicing.

Finnish Rusks

Rusks are toasts. Cut into fingers, they function as snacks, like biscotti. In larger pieces, they can be used as a base for eggs Benedict, eggs florentine, creamed fish, or sautéed mushrooms.

SMALL LOAF (1 POUND)	INGREDIENTS	LARGE LOAF (1½ POUNDS)
⅔ cup	milk	1 cup
¼ cup	honey	⅓ cup
1¼ teaspoons	active dry yeast	2 teaspoons
2 cups	bread flour	3 cups
½ teaspoon	salt	¾ teaspoon
¼ teaspoon	ground cardamom	½ teaspoon
2 tablespoons	vegetable oil	3 tablespoons

1. Scald the milk, stir in the honey, and let cool to room temperature.

2. Add the milk mixture and all remaining ingredients in the order suggested by your bread machine manual and process on the basic bread cycle according to the manufacturer's directions.

3. Preheat the oven to 200 degrees. Remove the bread from the machine and let cool completely. Slice into ½-inch rounds. Bake for 1 hour. Let cool. Store in tightly covered tins or wide-mouth jars.

NOTE: If you prefer melba thins, preheat the oven to 300 degrees. Slice the bread a scant ¼ inch thick and bake for 20 minutes, or until golden.

East African Sambosa

Traditionally in Kenya meat, spices, and peas are the filling for a bland dough that is shaped into a turnover and deep fried. This version is a little healthier and a lot easier. Sambosa bread makes a spicy main dish. Serve with crudités or vegetable soup during the Super Bowl or after your own touch football game.

SMALL LOAF (1 POUND)	INGREDIENTS	LARGE LOAF (1½ POUNDS)
¼ pound	ground beef round	6 ounces
1	garlic clove(s), minced	2
1 small	onion, chopped	1 medium
1½ teaspoons	active dry yeast	2 teaspoons
2 cups	bread flour	3 cups
1 teaspoon	salt	1¼ teaspoons
¼ teaspoon	ground cumin	½ teaspoon
¼ teaspoon	ground cardamom	½ teaspoon
¼ teaspoon	ground cloves	½ teaspoon
¼ teaspoon	grated nutmeg	½ teaspoon
¼ teaspoon	ground cinnamon	½ teaspoon
¼ teaspoon	ground black pepper	½ teaspoon
¾ cup	water	1 cup
¼ cup	frozen green peas	⅓ cup

1. In a large skillet, preferably nonstick, cook the beef, stirring to break up lumps of meat, until no longer pink, 3 to 5 minutes. Add the garlic and onion and cook until the onion is softened, 3 to 5 minutes longer. Let cool.

2. Add the cooled beef mixture and all remaining ingredients except the peas in the order suggested by your bread machine manual and process on the basic bread cycle according to the manufacturer's directions.

3. At the beeper (or at the end of the first kneading in the Panasonic or National), add the still-frozen peas. Eat warm or cool, cut into wedges instead of slices.

Hazelnut Bread and Biscotti

Biscotti are twice-baked cookies—a favorite Italian dessert. They are served with cappuccino, red wine, or hot chocolate, and they keep so well that you can always have a supply on hand.

SMALL LOAF (1 POUND)	INGREDIENTS	LARGE LOAF (1½ POUNDS)
1 teaspoon	active dry yeast	1½ teaspoons
1½ cups	bread flour	2¼ cups
½ cup	whole wheat flour	¾ cup
2 tablespoons	wheat germ	3 tablespoons
2 tablespoons	powdered milk	3 tablespoons
¼ cup	sugar	¼ cup plus 2 tablespoons
2 tablespoons	anise or fennel seeds	3 tablespoons
2 tablespoons	vegetable oil	3 tablespoons
¾ cup	water	1 cup plus 2 tablespoons
½ cup	chopped hazelnuts	¾ cup

1. Add all ingredients except the hazelnuts in the order suggested by your bread machine manual and process on the basic bread cycle according to the manufacturer's directions.

2. At the beeper (or at the end of the first kneading in the Panasonic or National), add the hazelnuts. Let cool or eat warm.

3. To make biscotti, preheat your oven to 350 degrees. Slice cooled bread ½ inch thick. Cut slices into fingers 1 inch wide. Place on baking sheet and toast for 15 to 20 minutes. The fresher the bread, the longer it needs to toast. Let cool and store in airtight containers or freeze.

Italian Cracked Wheat and Pepper Bread

Minestrone and vegetable soup taste even better with this spicy, crunchy bread, and it can make a fried egg sandwich a whole new experience. Toast slices and use as a base for eggs Benedict or rub with olive oil, cut into fingers, toast, and you will have a rustic, portable hors d'oeuvre.

SMALL LOAF (1 POUND)	INGREDIENTS	LARGE LOAF (1½ POUNDS)
1½ teaspoons	active dry yeast	2¼ teaspoons
1⅔ cups	bread flour	2½ cups
½ cup	cracked wheat	¾ cup
1 tablespoon	sugar	1½ tablespoons
2 tablespoons	wheat germ	3 tablespoons
½ teaspoon	coarsely cracked black pepper	¾ teaspoon
1 teaspoon	salt	1½ teaspoons
1 tablespoon	olive oil	1½ tablespoons
¾ cup plus 2 tablespoons	water	1¼ cups

Add all ingredients in the order suggested by your bread machine manual and process on the basic bread cycle according to the manufacturer's directions. Let the loaf cool before slicing.

Jamaican Coconut and Ginger Bread

If you cannot make it to the Caribbean, pretend you're there with a brunch of fresh tropical fruits, this coconut and ginger bread, and rum punch. Slice the bread into wedges or thick fingers instead of typical slices, and serve with curried eggs, or curried chicken, and a crisp salad.

SMALL LOAF (1 POUND)	INGREDIENTS	LARGE LOAF (1½ POUNDS)
¾ cup plus 2 tablespoons	milk	1¼ cups
2 tablespoons	unsalted butter	3 tablespoons
1½ tablespoons	honey	2 tablespoons
1¼ teaspoons	active dry yeast	2 teaspoons
2 cups	bread flour	3 cups
1 tablespoon	chopped fresh ginger	1½ tablespoons
½ teaspoon	salt	1 teaspoon
½ cup	flaked coconut	¾ cup

1. Scald the milk. Remove from the heat. Stir in butter and honey. Let cool to room temperature.

2. Add the milk mixture and all remaining ingredients except the coconut in the order suggested by your bread machine manual and process on the basic bread cycle according to the manufacturer's directions.

3. At the beeper (or at the end of the first kneading in the Panasonic or National), add the coconut. Let the bread cool before slicing.

Mocha Nut Bread

Plain or toasted, this is a good snack with milk or red wine. For dessert after an Italian dinner, serve poached pears or baked apples with toasted slices of the bread instead of cookies.

SMALL LOAF (1 POUND)	INGREDIENTS	LARGE LOAF (1½ POUNDS)
¾ cup plus 2 tablespoons	milk	1¼ cups
¼ cup	unsweetened cocoa powder	⅓ cup
2 teaspoons	instant espresso or coffee or decaf	1 tablespoon
3 tablespoons	unsalted butter	4 tablespoons
¼ cup	honey	¼ cup plus 2 tablespoons
¼ teaspoon	active dry yeast	2 teaspoons
2 cups	bread flour	3 cups
1 teaspoon	salt	1½ teaspoons
1	whole egg	1
0	egg yolk	1
¼ cup	walnuts or hazelnuts, coarsely chopped	⅓ cup

1. Scald the milk; remove from the heat. Add the cocoa and instant coffee and stir until dissolved. Stir in the butter and honey. The mixture should be close to room temperature; if not, let it cool until it is.

2. Add cocoa mixture and all remaining ingredients except the nuts in the order suggested by your bread machine manual and process on the basic bread cycle according to the manufacturer's directions.

Mozzarella and Sun-Dried Tomato Bread

If you want to flatter your meat loaf, put it between slices of this toothsome bread. Cold roast beef or turkey or sliced eggs also will benefit from the slightly salty yet creamy taste of this tender loaf. It is also good with a crisp filling of thinly sliced raw vegetables: cucumber, radish, endive, turnip, or pepper.

SMALL LOAF (1 POUND)	INGREDIENTS	LARGE LOAF (1½ POUNDS)
1½ teaspoons	active dry yeast	2½ teaspoons
1¾ cups	bread flour	2¾ cups
1 tablespoon	sugar	1½ tablespoons
1 teaspoon	salt	1½ teaspoons
1 tablespoon	olive oil	1½ tablespoons
⅓ cup	chopped sun-dried tomatoes	½ cup
½ cup	water	¾ cup
⅓ cup	cubed mozzarella cheese	½ cup

1. Add all ingredients except the mozzarella cheese in the order suggested by your bread machine manual and process on the basic bread cycle according to the manufacturer's directions.

2. At the beeper (or at the end of the first kneading in the Panasonic or National), add the mozzarella cheese.

Naan-Flavored Bread

Naan is a flat bread from India. This version is high and light, but retains the subtle taste and spirit of naan. Though not spicy, it is flavorful and tastes best with a hot Indian curry, Moroccan tagine, or Texas chili.

SMALL LOAF (1 POUND)	INGREDIENTS	LARGE LOAF (1½ POUNDS)
1 tablespoon	chopped garlic	1½ tablespoons
2 tablespoons	chopped onion	3 tablespoons
2 tablespoons	vegetable oil	3 tablespoons
1¼ teaspoons	active dry yeast	2¼ teaspoons
2 cups	bread flour	3 cups
½ tablespoon	sugar	2 teaspoons
1¼ teaspoons	salt	1¾ teaspoons
½ cup	plain yogurt	¾ cup
⅓ cup	water	½ cup
2 tablespoons	unhulled sesame seeds	3 tablespoons

1. In a small skillet, cook the garlic and onion over medium heat until golden, 5 to 7 minutes. Let cool to room temperature.

2. Add the sautéed onion and garlic and all remaining ingredients except the sesame seeds in the order suggested by your bread machine manual and process on the basic bread cycle according to the manufacturer's directions.

3. At the beeper (or at the end of the first kneading in the Panasonic or National), add the sesame seeds.

Oriental Sesame Bread

This slightly spicy bread partners barbecued spareribs—Chinese or Texas style— or any broiled meat. Toast slightly and top with sliced teriyaki steak or chicken.

SMALL LOAF (1 POUND)	INGREDIENTS	LARGE LOAF (1½ POUNDS)
2 tablespoons	unhulled sesame seeds	3 tablespoons
1¼ teaspoons	active dry yeast	1¾ teaspoons
2 cups	bread flour	3 cups
¼ cup	cracked wheat	⅓ cup
1 tablespoon	sugar	1½ tablespoons
1 teaspoon	salt	1½ teaspoons
¼ teaspoon	ground ginger	½ teaspoon
1 tablespoon	chopped red bell pepper	1½ tablespoons
2 tablespoons	chopped scallions	3 tablespoons
2 tablespoons	Asian sesame oil	3 tablespoons
1 tablespoon	soy sauce	1½ tablespoons
¾ cup	water	1 cup plus 2 tablespoons

1. In a medium skillet, preferably nonstick, toast the sesame seeds over medium heat, shaking the pan, until they are fragrant and lightly browned, 2 to 3 minutes. Set aside.

2. Add all ingredients except the sesame seeds in the order suggested by your bread machine manual and process on the basic bread cycle according to the manufacturer's directions.

3. At the beeper (or at the end of the first kneading in the Panasonic or National), add the toasted sesame seeds.

Parisian Currant Rye Bread

The sweetness of currants, sour of rye, and spice of caraway make a bread so intensely flavored that it is best eaten on its own in thin slices, with just a slim coating of butter. In France, this bread is found only in the best traditional bakeries.

SMALL LOAF (1 POUND)	INGREDIENTS	LARGE LOAF (1½ POUNDS)
1 teaspoon	active dry yeast	1½ teaspoons
1⅓ cups	bread flour	2¼ cups
⅔ cup	rye flour	1 cup
1 teaspoon	salt	1½ teaspoons
1 tablespoon	caraway seeds	1½ tablespoons
⅔ cup	sourdough starter (page 7) *	1 cup
½ cup	water	¾ cup
½ cup	currants	¾ cup

1. Add all ingredients except the currants in the order suggested by your bread machine manual and process on the basic bread cycle according to the manufacturer's directions.

2. At the beeper (or at the end of the first kneading in the Panasonic or National), add the currants. Let the loaf cool. Slice very thin.

* After measuring out what is needed for this recipe, be sure to replenish your sourdough starter with equal amounts of flour and water.

Peanut and Curry Bread

Inspired by my love of Indian food, this bread goes beautifully with all kinds of curries. Spread with cream cheese or yogurt and chutney or sandwiched with chicken or chutney mayonnaise, it is excellent for tea.

SMALL LOAF (1 POUND)	INGREDIENTS	LARGE LOAF (1½ POUNDS)
1½ teaspoons	active dry yeast	2¼ teaspoons
1 cup	bread flour	1½ cups
1 cup	whole wheat flour	1½ cups
1 teaspoon	salt	1½ teaspoons
1 tablespoon	sugar	1½ tablespoons
1½ teaspoons	curry powder	2¼ teaspoons
1 tablespoon	grated orange zest	1½ tablespoons
¼ cup	flaked coconut	⅓ cup
1 tablespoon	vegetable oil	2 tablespoons
2 tablespoons	peanut butter	3 tablespoons
¾ cup plus 2 tablespoons	water	1¼ cups

Add all ingredients in the order suggested by your bread machine manual and process on the basic bread cycle according to the manufacturer's directions.

Pepperoni Pecorino Bread

This is an antipasto in a loaf. The cheese and meat are already in the bread. All you need are some marinated vegetables and red wine to have a party. Or serve with a green salad for lunch.

SMALL LOAF (1 POUND)	INGREDIENTS	LARGE LOAF (1½ POUNDS)
1½ teaspoons	active dry yeast	2¼ teaspoons
2 cups	bread flour	3 cups
2 tablespoons	wheat bran	3 tablespoons
1 tablespoon	sugar	1½ tablespoons
1 teaspoon	salt	1½ teaspoons
¼ teaspoon	ground black pepper	½ teaspoon
1	egg	1
1 tablespoon	vegetable oil	1½ tablespoons
⅔ cup	water	1 cup
½ cup	grated Pecorino, Romano, or Parmesan cheese	¾ cup
¼ cup	diced pepperoni, salami, or ham	⅓ cup

1. Add all ingredients except the pepperoni in the order suggested by your bread machine manual and process on the basic bread cycle according to the manufacturer's directions.

2. At the beeper (or at the end of the first kneading in the Panasonic or National), add the pepperoni, salami, or ham.

Potato Bread Dauphinois

A very rich, creamy French potato gratin suggested this bread. I've kept all of the taste, but not all of the cream and calories. Serve warm or cooled with beef stew or a roast, or use it for sandwiches. Any leftover potatoes can be mashed for the bread. And it is sensational with French onion or homemade vegetable soup on a cold winter night.

SMALL LOAF (1 POUND)	INGREDIENTS	LARGE LOAF (1½ POUNDS)
1 teaspoon	active dry yeast	1½ teaspoons
2 cups	bread flour	3 cups
2 tablespoons	cracked wheat	3 tablespoons
1 tablespoon	sugar	1½ tablespoons
1 teaspoon	salt	1½ teaspoons
¼ teaspoon	ground black pepper	½ teaspoon
1	garlic clove(s), minced	2
1 tablespoon	vegetable oil	1½ tablespoons
½ cup	mashed potato	¾ cup
½ cup	plain yogurt	¾ cup
¼ cup	water	½ cup
½ cup	grated Swiss cheese	¾ cup

1. Add all ingredients except the Swiss cheese in the order suggested by your bread machine manual and process on the basic bread cycle according to the manufacturer's directions.

2. At the beeper (or at the end of the first kneading in the Panasonic or National), add the Swiss cheese.

Scandinavian Rye Bread

For canapés or for Danish open-faced sandwiches, cut this bread into thin slices and top with smoked salmon, fish salad, or sliced hard-boiled egg and anchovies. Slice the bread thicker for regular sandwiches and fill with cold meat loaf, ham, or muenster cheese. It is also marvelous untoasted with butter or jam for breakfast.

SMALL LOAF (1 POUND)	INGREDIENTS	LARGE LOAF (1½ POUNDS)
1¾ teaspoons	active dry yeast	2½ teaspoons
1⅓ cups	bread flour	2 cups
1 cup	rye flour	1½ cups
½ teaspoon	salt	¾ teaspoon
1½ tablespoons	caraway seeds	2 tablespoons
1 tablespoon	vegetable oil	1½ tablespoons
2 tablespoons	unsulphured molasses	3 tablespoons
1 tablespoon	vinegar	1½ tablespoons
⅓ cup	water	½ cup
⅓ cup	room-temperature beer	½ cup

Add all ingredients in the order suggested by your bread machine manual and process on the basic bread cycle according to the manufacturer's directions.

Pesto Bread

Save this recipe for summer, when fresh basil is plentiful and pungent. Serve with pasta, minestrone, gazpacho, or barbecue. For a sandwich, fill with cold grilled meat or chicken. Turn any leftovers into croutons and float in hot or cold vegetable soup.

SMALL LOAF (1 POUND)	INGREDIENTS	LARGE LOAF (1½ POUNDS)
¼ cup	fresh basil leaves	⅓ cup
½	garlic clove	1
1 tablespoon	grated Parmesan cheese	1½ tablespoons
1 tablespoon	walnuts	1½ tablespoons
2 tablespoons	olive oil	3 tablespoons
1¼ teaspoons	active dry yeast	2 teaspoons
2 cups	bread flour	3 cups
¼ cup	wheat bran	⅓ cup
1 tablespoon	sugar	1½ tablespoons
1 teaspoon	salt	1½ teaspoons
½ cup	water	¾ cup

1. In a food processor or by hand, grind the basil, garlic, grated cheese, walnuts, and olive oil into a thick paste. This is the pesto.

2. Add the pesto and all remaining ingredients in the order suggested by your bread machine manual and process on the basic bread cycle according to the manufacturer's directions.

Pizza Bread

Top or fill with mozzarella cheese and grill for the taste of pizza with little fuss.
This bread travels much better than its namesake, and it will not burn the roof of
your mouth. It also makes a tasty meat loaf or cold roast chicken sandwich.

SMALL LOAF (1 POUND)	INGREDIENTS	LARGE LOAF (1½ POUNDS)
1½ teaspoons	active dry yeast	2¼ teaspoons
2 cups	bread flour	3 cups
2 tablespoons	wheat germ	3 tablespoons
1 teaspoon	salt	1½ teaspoons
1 tablespoon	minced garlic	1½ tablespoons
1 tablespoon	grated Parmesan cheese	1½ tablespoons
2 tablespoons	olive oil	3 tablespoons
½ cup	tomato sauce, tomato puree, or marinara sauce	¾ cup
⅓ cup	water	½ cup

Add all ingredients in the order suggested by your bread machine manual and process
on the basic bread cycle according to the manufacturer's directions.

Provençal Olive and Thyme Bread

I am particularly fond of this bread with roast lamb, baked or broiled fish, or with a salad Niçoise. Unadorned slices are just right with a basket of cherry tomatoes and goat cheese with a glass of white wine or cider.

SMALL LOAF (1 POUND)	INGREDIENTS	LARGE LOAF (1½ POUNDS)
1 teaspoon	active dry yeast	1¼ teaspoons
2 cups	bread flour	3 cups
¼ cup	whole wheat flour	⅓ cup
1 tablespoon	sugar	1½ tablespoons
¼ teaspoon	salt	½ teaspoon
1 teaspoon	dried thyme leaves	1½ teaspoons
2 tablespoons	olive oil	3 tablespoons
¾ cup plus 2 tablespoons	water	1¼ cups
¼ cup	pitted and chopped black olives	⅓ cup

1. Add all ingredients except the black olives in the order suggested by your bread machine manual and process on the basic bread cycle according to the manufacturer's directions.

2. At the beeper (or at the end of the first kneading in the Panasonic or National), add the olives. Let the loaf cool before slicing.

Swedish Limpa

From one bakery to the next in Bay Ridge, the old Scandinavian neighborhood near the Brooklyn waterfront, we tasted Limpa bread. Each bakery had a slightly different version, but they all tasted of spices and rye. This recipe is the perfect bread to serve with a smorgasbord of assorted fish and meats. It is traditionally the bread that supports Danish open-faced sandwiches topped with smoked salmon or baby shrimp and dill, thinly sliced ham garnished with gherkins, or steak tartare.

SMALL LOAF (1 POUND)	INGREDIENTS	LARGE LOAF (1½ POUNDS)
1½ teaspoons	active dry yeast	2¼ teaspoons
1¼ cups	bread flour	1¾ cups plus 2 tablespoons
1 cup	rye flour	1½ cups
1 tablespoon	brown sugar	1½ tablespoons
1 teaspoon	fennel seeds	1½ teaspoons
¼ teaspoon	ground cardamom	⅜ teaspoon
1 teaspoon	salt	1½ teaspoons
1 tablespoon	grated or chopped orange zest	1½ tablespoons
1 tablespoon	vegetable oil	1½ tablespoons
¾ cup plus 2 tablespoons	water	1⅓ cups

Add all ingredients in the order suggested by your bread machine manual and process on the basic bread cycle according to the manufacturer's directions. Let the loaf cool. Slice thin.

Scotch Egg Revisited

Scotch eggs are traditional English pub food, made by encasing boiled eggs in sausage meat, coating them with bread crumbs and deep frying until golden. Turning the flavors into a loaf eliminates the frying and divides the egg and meat among four or more people.

Cut the loaf into wedges so that each piece contains a wedge of egg. It makes a good breakfast for a canoe trip or in a campground. As an hors d'oeuvre, serve with curried mayonnaise. This was our dog's favorite—he ate the whole loaf as soon as our backs were turned.

SMALL LOAF (1 POUND)	INGREDIENTS	LARGE LOAF (1½ POUNDS)
½ cup	sausage	¾ cup
1	shelled hard-boiled egg(s)	2
1 teaspoon	active dry yeast	1½ teaspoons
1 cup plus 2 tablespoons	bread flour	1⅔ cups
1 cup	whole wheat flour	1½ cups
1 tablespoon	sugar	1½ tablespoons
1 teaspoon	salt	1½ teaspoons
2 tablespoons	powdered milk	3 tablespoons
1 tablespoon	vegetable oil	1½ tablespoons
¾ cup plus 1 tablespoon	water	1¼ cups

1. Remove the casings from the sausage. Crumble into a medium skillet, preferably nonstick, and cook over medium heat, stirring until brown, about 5 minutes. Drain well.

2. Add cooked sausage and all remaining ingredients except the cooked egg(s) in the order suggested by your bread machine manual and process on the basic bread cycle according to the manufacturer's directions.

3. One hour before the end of the baking cycle, while the dough still has time to rise, carefully push the egg(s) into the dough vertically. Be very gentle, deflating the dough as little as possible. Let the machine finish the baking cycle. Remove carefully and cut into wedges.

Welsh Raisin Bread (Bara Brith)

This is a whole wheat rendition of Judith and Evan Jones's family recipe for Bara Brith from their book, The Book of Bread. *Orange and spices enliven this breakfast or sandwich bread, making it a tea or coffee cake, too. The loaf is lovely toasted, almost as if the marmalade were already spread on it.*

SMALL LOAF (1 POUND)	INGREDIENTS	LARGE LOAF (1½ POUNDS)
¾ cup	milk	1 cup plus 2 tablespoons
⅓ cup	currants	½ cup
⅓ cup	golden raisins	½ cup
1 cup	hot strongly brewed tea	1½ cups
1½ teaspoons	active dry yeast	2¼ teaspoons
1 cup	bread flour	1½ cups
1 cup	whole wheat flour	1½ cups
2 tablespoons	brown sugar	3 tablespoons
2 tablespoons	unsalted butter	3 tablespoons
¼ teaspoon	ground cinnamon	½ teaspoon
¼ teaspoon	grated nutmeg	¼ teaspoon
⅛ teaspoon	ground cloves	¼ teaspoon
½ teaspoon	salt	¾ teaspoon
¼ cup	chopped candied orange zest (page 136)	⅓ cup

1. Scald the milk. Let cool to room temperature. Soak the currants and yellow raisins in the tea for 10 minutes, until soft and plumped; drain.

2. Add the milk and all remaining ingredients except the currants and golden raisins in the order suggested by your bread machine manual and process on the basic bread cycle according to the manufacturer's directions.

3. At the beeper (or at the end of the first kneading in the Panasonic or National), add the currants and golden raisins.

Chapter Six

Shaped Breads from Machine Dough

Now let your imagination and creativity take over with breads first kneaded on the dough cycle, shaped by hand, and baked in the oven —when you have the time. The bread machine takes the drudgery out of kneading the dough, but you still have the fun of sculpting and decorating it.

Although these recipes are not as easy as those in other chapters, the taste and rustic beauty of these wreaths and braids, flat breads and gooey buns are well worth the effort. Some, like the pizza and filled breads, are meals in themselves. Others, like the Greek Easter Bread and Swedish Christmas Wreath, are as good looking as they are good tasting.

Many of the doughs can be made ahead and have their final rising and baking just before being served. Sticky buns and hot cross buns kneaded and shaped the night before fill the house with sweet and spicy smells as they bake for the freshest of Christmas or Easter breakfasts.

If you ever wanted to sculpt or paint, here is your chance. Dough is the superb artistic medium since it is so tactile, and everything you create will be consumed, encouraging only further creation. Roll dough into a canvas for decorating with color and shapes, or sculpt it into traditional spirals and wreaths or original designs.

Have a wonderful time.

Crusty French Baguettes

This is the real thing—as good as anything you ever bought in a bakery, but better because it is fresher. Eat plain, with butter, or make the best sandwich ever, with just about anything.

Yield: 2 baguettes

1½ teaspoons	active dry yeast
2½ cups	bread flour
1 teaspoon	salt
1 cup	water
1 tablespoon	cornmeal

1. Add the yeast, bread flour, salt, and water in the order suggested by your bread machine manual and process on the dough cycle according to the manufacturer's directions.

2. At the end of the dough cycle, remove the dough from the machine and divide into 2 equal pieces. Form each piece into a round, pressing to break any air bubbles. Place the rounds on a lightly greased plate or cookie sheet, leaving room for the balls of dough to double in size. Cover with a clean bowl or kitchen towel and let rise about 20 minutes in a draft-free but not hot place. If your kitchen is chilly, the dough might need another 5 or 10 minutes to double in size. If you press the dough lightly with your finger and the mark remains, the dough is ready. If the indentation springs out again, the dough needs to rise longer.

3. Preheat the oven to 375 degrees. Roll each ball of dough into a rope as long as a cookie sheet, French bread mold, or any other long baking pan. Sprinkle the cornmeal on the pan. Place the baguettes on the tray at least 4 inches apart. Let rise again, covered, until double in size, about 30 minutes.

4. When the dough has doubled, spray or paint gently with cold water. Slit the top diagonally several times with a sharp knife or a single-edge razor. Bake 25 to 30 minutes, spraying with water once or twice more. *Voilà!*

Barbecued Fresh Tomato Pizza

Summer means never turning on your oven and never slaving over a hot stove stirring sauce; it always means having baskets of really red tomatoes. Once you make the dough in your bread machine, you can do the rest outdoors. You can serve this to a crowd as part of a buffet or as the first course for a barbecue. Once you get used to the foibles of your own grill, this will be as easy as it is beautiful and bright.

Yield: 2 medium or 1 large pizza

1½ teaspoons	active dry yeast
2 cups	bread flour
1 teaspoon	salt
2 tablespoons	vegetable oil
¾ cup plus 2 tablespoons	water
2 pounds	ripe summer tomatoes
2 tablespoons	cornmeal
2 tablespoons	olive oil
3 tablespoons	grated Parmesan cheese
2 tablespoons	chopped fresh basil

1. Add the yeast, bread flour, salt, vegetable oil, and water in the order suggested by your bread machine manual and process on the dough cycle according to the manufacturer's directions.

2. Slice the tomatoes ¼ inch thick. Light the barbecue and set the grill rack at least 6 inches from the heat. Line a cookie sheet or two medium pizza pans with a double thickness of foil, turning up the ends of the foil. Be sure the tray is no bigger than the top of your grill. Sprinkle the cornmeal on the foil.

3. When the dough cycle ends, remove the dough from the machine. Roll out the dough on a floured board with a floured rolling pin until very thin (almost ⅛ inch thick). The large pizza should be 18 inches in diameter, the two smaller ones 13 inches each. Place the dough on foil-lined trays. Spread the sliced tomatoes over the dough. Drizzle the olive oil over the tomatoes and sprinkle on the cheese and basil.

4. Carefully pull the foil holding the pizza off the tray and onto the grill. Cover the grill and check the pizza after 10 minutes. If the crust is browned on the bottom, the pizza is ready. If not, grill a few minutes longer. Slide the pizza on the foil back onto the tray and serve hot. It isn't bad at room temperature either.

Pizza Rustica

This is a great dish for a party. Invite guests over or take a loaf with you to a potluck supper or a picnic at Tanglewood. This filled bread is rustic and elegant at the same time, easy to make ahead and reheat, and perfectly fine at room temperature.

Yield: 1 (9-inch) filled pizza, serving 4 to 6

DOUGH

1¼ teaspoons	active dry yeast
2 cups	bread flour
3 tablespoons	sugar
1 teaspoon	salt
3 tablespoons	vegetable oil
¼ teaspoon	freshly ground black pepper
⅔ cup	water

FILLING

1	egg
1 cup	ricotta cheese
¼ teaspoon	freshly ground black pepper
1 tablespoon	grated Parmesan cheese
¼ pound	Italian salami or mortadella
½ cup	shredded mozzarella cheese
½ cup	sliced roasted red pepper

1. Add all ingredients for the dough in the order suggested by your bread machine manual and process on the dough cycle according to the manufacturer's directions.

2. At the end of the dough cycle, remove the dough from the machine. Preheat the oven to 375 degrees.

3. On a floured surface with a floured rolling pin, roll out the dough into a large circle no more than ¼ inch thick. Line a 9-inch pie plate (preferably glass) with the dough, leaving at least a 4-inch overhang all around.

4. For the filling, beat the egg in a large bowl. Add the ricotta cheese, Parmesan cheese, and black pepper; blend well. Spread one third of the salami or mortadella over the dough. Top with one half of the ricotta mixture. Sprinkle on one half of the mozzarella and roasted pepper. Repeat the layers, ending with the last of the meat. Pull the edges of the dough up over the filling. Pinch and press the edges of the dough together in the center to seal. Let the filled pizza rise for 15 minutes.

5. Bake the pizza rustica 30 minutes (This dish can be made up to a day in advance, refrigerated, and rewarmed.)

Focaccia

Focaccia is a great snack; it can be cut up and served as an hors d'oeuvre, and it goes well with soups and pasta. Instead of rosemary, try basil or thyme, or top the bread with anchovies or olives.

Yield: 2 medium or 1 large flat bread

1½ teaspoons	active dry yeast
2½ cups	bread flour
1 teaspoon	salt
2 tablespoons	vegetable oil
1 cup	water
1 tablespoon	cornmeal
1 tablespoon	olive oil
1 teaspoon	coarse kosher salt
2 teaspoons	dried rosemary

1. Add the yeast, flour, salt, vegetable oil, and water in the order suggested by your bread machine manual and process on the dough cycle according to the manufacturer's directions.

2. At the end of the dough cycle, remove the dough from the machine. Preheat the oven to 450 degrees.

3. Cut the dough in half. Press out each half into a circle about 9 inches in diameter. Transfer to a pizza tray or cookie sheet dusted with the cornmeal. Cover with a clean kitchen towel and let rise 5 minutes. Press fingers into dough to create dimples. (You can also make one large focaccia that will cover a whole 11-by-16-inch pan.)

4. Drizzle half the olive oil over each focaccia and sprinkle half the salt and half the rosemary on each. Bake for 15 minutes, or until golden.

Sally Lunn Bread

If there was a real Sally Lunn, she did not make it into the English history books; only her bread recipe remains. Still warm, with a dab of strawberry jam, it is irresistible. A drizzle of caramel sauce or sautéed apples can transform this bread or breakfast cake into dessert.

Yield: 2 small or 1 large bundt-shaped cake

1½ teaspoons	active dry yeast
1¾ cups plus 2 tablespoons	bread flour
3 tablespoons	sugar
1 teaspoon	salt
4 tablespoons	butter
2	eggs
½ cup	milk or light cream

1. Add all ingredients in the order suggested by your bread machine manual and process on the dough cycle according to the manufacturer's directions.

2. At the end of the dough cycle, remove the dough from the machine. Preheat the oven to 350 degrees. Grease a 10-inch tube pan, an angel food cake pan, or bundt pan.

3. On a floured surface, roll the dough into a rope, place in the greased pan, and pinch the ends together. Cover and let rise in a draft-free place for 30 minutes, or until doubled in size.

4. Bake 40 to 45 minutes, or until the bread is golden brown and sounds hollow when tapped. Let cool 10 minutes before turning out of the pan. Cool completely before slicing.

Filled Breads

These breads can be as rustic or as refined as you choose, depending on the filling and decoration. At a very snazzy Connecticut summer wedding under a tent, the breads were filled with salami and cheese and decorated with leaves made from dough scraps. The only other food was strawberries and crudités plus endless champagne and the wedding cake. We danced all night.

Yield: a 2-pound loaf; enough for 4 as a main course, or 6 to 8 as a snack

---

DOUGH

1¼ teaspoons	active dry yeast
1¾ cups	bread flour
1 tablespoon	sugar
1 teaspoon	salt
1 tablespoon	vegetable oil
½ cup	sourdough starter (page 7) *
½ cup	water

FILLING

¼ pound	salami
¼ pound	provolone or mozzarella cheese, sliced
¼ cup	roasted red pepper, cut into strips
	or
¼ pound	smoked turkey
¼ pound	Swiss cheese, grated
4	frozen asparagus spears

---

	or
½ pound	frozen broccoli pieces
¼ pound	Cheddar cheese, grated
2 tablespoons	chopped sun-dried tomatoes

GLAZE

1	egg, beaten

1. Add all ingredients for the dough in the order suggested by your bread machine manual and process on the dough cycle according to the manufacturer's directions.

2. When the dough cycle ends, remove the dough from the machine. Preheat the oven to 375 degrees.

3. With a floured rolling pin on a floured surface, roll the dough into an 8-by-15-inch rectangle. (If you want to decorate the bread, cut off a small bit of dough and reserve.) Place the dough on a piece of floured wax paper or plastic wrap to make it easier to work with. Spread any of the fillings—or your own combination with the same proportions—down the center of the dough lengthwise, leaving a 1-inch margin all around. With the help of the plastic wrap or wax paper, pick up the long sides and press them together, pinching to seal; tuck in well the short ends to form a neat package. Turn, seam side down, onto a greased baking sheet. Brush lightly with the beaten egg. Decorate with leaves or strips cut from the reserved dough. Let bread rise for 30 minutes.

4. Bake 30 minutes, or until brown.

* After measuring out what is needed for this recipe, be sure to replenish your sourdough starter with equal amounts of flour and water.

Swedish Christmas Wreath

If you want your house to smell like Christmas, bake this bread. It tastes and looks festive. Serve with eggnog or glugg—Swedish hot wine punch—during the holidays. Spiral ribbon around the wreath and give it as a gift.

Yield: 1 wreath-shaped bread, serving 8 or more

DOUGH

⅔ cup	milk
1½ teaspoons	active dry yeast
2 cups	bread flour
3 tablespoons	sugar
½ teaspoon	salt
½ teaspoon	ground cardamom
1	egg
4 tablespoons	unsalted butter

FILLING AND GLAZE

½ cup	raisins
½ cup	citron or candied lemon zest (page 136)
½ cup plus 2 tablespoons	sliced blanched almonds
1	egg, beaten

1. Scald the milk. Let cool to room temperature.

2. Add the cooled milk and all remaining ingredients for the dough in the order suggested by your bread machine manual and process on the dough cycle according to the manufacturer's directions.

3. At the end of the dough cycle, remove the dough from the machine. Preheat the oven to 350 degrees.

4. On a floured surface with a floured rolling pin, roll out the dough into a rectangle at least 24 inches long and 6 inches wide. Spread the raisins, citron or candied lemon peel, and ½ cup of the almonds over the dough, leaving a ½-inch margin all around. Roll up tightly from a long side, jelly-roll fashion. You will have a long, thick rope. With a very sharp knife, beginning 1 inch from the end, slice down the center of the rope lengthwise, stopping 1 inch short of the other end. Hold one end of the dough in each hand. Twist the dough in opposite directions. Arrange this long twist in a circle on a greased cookie sheet. Pinch the ends together to form a wreath.

5. Brush the beaten egg over the wreath and sprinkle on the remaining 2 tablespoons almonds. Let rise ½ hour in a draft-free place until double in size.

6. Bake 30 minutes, or until the bread sounds hollow when tapped.

Chinese Steamed Meat Buns

Serve as a separate course for a formal Chinese dinner or as part of dim sum—
Chinese tidbits—or as part of a meal with a dish of stir-fried vegetables.

Yield: 12 buns

DOUGH

1 teaspoon	active dry yeast
1¾ cups	bread flour
1½ teaspoons	sugar
1 tablespoon	vegetable oil
½ cup	water

FILLING

½ pound	ground pork, turkey, or beef
1	scallion, chopped
1	garlic clove, minced
1	egg white
1 tablespoon	soy sauce
1 tablespoon	dry sherry
⅛ teaspoon	salt
⅛ teaspoon	ground black pepper
1 tablespoon	Asian sesame oil

1. Add all ingredients for the dough in the order suggested by your bread machine manual and process on the dough cycle according to the manufacturer's directions.

2. To make the filling, mix together the ground meat, scallion, garlic, egg white, soy sauce, sherry, salt, pepper, and sesame oil.

3. When the dough cycle ends, remove the dough from the machine and divide it into 12 equal pieces. Roll each piece into a thin circle about 5 inches in diameter. Put about 1 tablespoon of the filling in the center of each circle. Pull the edges of the dough up and around the filling, pleating the dough as it meets in the center to form a pouch. Pinch the dough closed. Repeat with the remaining circles. Let the buns rise 30 minutes, top side down, on a greased plate, spaced about 1 inch apart so they will not touch when they rise.

4. Use a bamboo steamer. If you do not have a steamer, improvise one by setting a heatproof dish or pie plate on a tin can with the bottom and top removed in a large frying pan or wok filled with 1 inch water. The plate should be about 1 inch smaller in width than the frying pan or wok to let the steam come up over the buns. The buns must sit above the boiling water, not in it.

5. Bring the water to a boil. Invert the dumplings onto the heatproof plate, which must be greased. Place the plate on top of the can in the steamer, cover the steamer, and steam the buns over medium heat 20 minutes. Serve hot, with soy sauce for dipping.

Hot Cross Buns

In England, hot cross buns, which are soft and sweet, appear on Good Friday, but in the United States, fortunately, they are a tradition throughout Lent. No one will stop you from eating them year round, either.

Yield: 12 hot cross buns

DOUGH

2 teaspoons	active dry yeast
2½ cups	bread flour
⅓ cup	sugar
½ teaspoon	salt
1 tablespoon	grated lemon zest
2½ tablespoons	unsalted butter
2	eggs
1 cup	water
½ cup	golden raisins
½ cup	currants

GLAZE

½ cup	confectioners' sugar
1 tablespoon	lemon juice

1. Add all ingredients for the dough except the golden raisins and currants in the order suggested by your bread machine manual and process on the dough cycle according to the manufacturer's directions.

2. At the beeper (or at the end of the first kneading in the Panasonic or National), add the raisins and currants.

3. At the end of the dough cycle, remove the dough from the machine. Preheat the oven to 350 degrees. Divide the fruited dough into 12 pieces. If the dough begins to stick, flour your hands. Roll each piece into a ball. On a greased baking sheet, arrange the balls of dough in 3 rows of 4 each, leaving at least 1 inch between buns. Cover with a clean kitchen towel and let rise in a draft-free place for 30 minutes, or until doubled in size.

4. Bake 15 minutes, or until the buns are golden brown. Remove from the oven. For the glaze, mix the confectioners' sugar and lemon juice until smooth. Dribble the glaze in a line across the warm buns. Make another line perpendicular to the first to create a cross shape on each bun.

Après-Ski Onion Kuchen

This recipe is adapted from a traditional Swiss after-ski snack. With red wine or hot cider, it will warm any cold skier or skater. If the baker skis, too, the kuchen can be prepared ahead and reheated for 15 minutes in a 350 degree oven.

Yield: 1 large kuchen

DOUGH

1½ teaspoons	active dry yeast
1½ cups	bread flour
1 cup	whole wheat flour
2 tablespoons	sugar
1 teaspoon	salt
2 tablespoons	vegetable oil
1	egg
1 cup	water

TOPPING

---

1 cup	paper-thin slices of potato
2 cups	ricotta cheese
1 cup	paper-thin slices of onion
¼ teaspoon	coarsely ground black pepper
½ teaspoon	kosher salt

1. Add all ingredients for the dough in the order suggested by your bread machine manual and process on the dough cycle according to the manufacturer's directions.

2. Meanwhile, cook the potato slices in a medium saucepan of boiling water for 3 minutes to soften slightly; drain well.

3. When the dough cycle ends, remove the dough from the machine. Preheat the oven to 350 degrees. On a floured surface with a floured rolling pin, roll out the dough into a 12-by-16-inch rectangle. Spread the ricotta cheese over the dough. Separate the onion into rings and sprinkle onion rings, potatoes, pepper, and the salt over the ricotta.

4. Slide the dough onto a large greased cookie sheet. If you do not have a large enough sheet, line the oven rack with a double layer of greased aluminum foil and place the dough on top of it. Bake 20 to 25 minutes, until the onions look crisp and lightly charred. Cut into squares and serve hot.

Onion Poppy Seed Flat Bread

Could there be a more popular and less expensive party and snack food? And it is full of fiber, too. Eat by breaking off crisp pieces and munching them. Break leftovers into pieces and store in airtight containers.

Yield: 4 flat breads

DOUGH

1½ teaspoons	active dry yeast
1 cup	bread flour
1 cup	whole wheat flour
¼ cup	cracked wheat
1 tablespoon	sugar
½ teaspoon	salt
2 tablespoons	vegetable oil
1 cup	water

TOPPING

1	egg, beaten
1 cup	minced onions
¼ cup	sesame seeds
¼ cup	poppy seeds

1. Add all ingredients for the dough in the order suggested by your bread machine manual and process on the dough cycle according to the manufacturer's directions.
2. At the end of the dough cycle, remove the dough from the machine. Preheat the oven to 400 degrees.
3. Divide the dough into 4 pieces. On a floured surface with a floured rolling pin, roll out each piece into a very thin 8-by-10-inch rectangle. Place 2 rectangles each on 2 lightly greased baking sheets.* Brush with beaten egg. Sprinkle one quarter of the topping ingredients over each rectangle.
4. Bake the flat breads 10 minutes, or until golden brown. Since the dough is so thin, it will burn quickly, so watch carefully.

* If only one rectangle at a time will fit on your baking sheets, form and bake the breads in batches.

Whole Wheat Pizza

The cheese on this pizza will be bubbling and the crust will be crisp and just as thin or thick as you like it. On top of that, the pizza will take less time to make than it would if you ordered it and had it delivered. Can it be gooey, delicious, and wholesome too? Yes—when you make it yourself.

Yield: 1 large, 2 medium, or 4 small (individual) pizzas

DOUGH

1½ teaspoons	active dry yeast
1 cup	bread flour
1 cup	whole wheat flour
1 tablespoon	sugar
1 teaspoon	salt
2 tablespoons	vegetable oil
¾ cup plus 2 tablespoons	water

TOPPING

1½ cups	spaghetti or tomato sauce or tomato puree
½ teaspoon	dried oregano
½ teaspoon	dried basil
1½ cups	shredded mozzarella cheese
1 tablespoon	cornmeal

1. Add all ingredients for the dough in the order suggested by your bread machine manual and process on the dough cycle according to the manufacturer's directions.

2. When the dough cycle ends, remove the dough from the machine. Preheat the oven to 450 degrees.

3. Make 1 large, 2 medium, or 4 individual pizzas. On a floured surface with a floured rolling pin, roll out the dough until it is less than ¼ inch thick. The large pizza will be about 15 inches in diameter or a rectangle about 12 by 18 inches; the medium will be about 10 inches in diameter; the individual about 7 inches in diameter. Spread the sauce over the dough. Sprinkle on the oregano, basil, and cheese. Slide the pizza onto a large cookie sheet or pizza pan dusted with the cornmeal.

4. Bake about 15 minutes, or until the cheese is bubbling and the crust is brown.

Monkey Bread Pull-Aparts

This is good sit-down brunch or on-the-run food. Half the fun is pulling apart the balls of caramelized sweet dough. Wrap the whole bread in clear cellophane and tie with a ribbon for an impressive gift.

Yield: 1 large bread, serving 8

DOUGH

1½ teaspoons	active dry yeast
1¼ cups	bread flour
1 cup	whole wheat flour
3 tablespoons	sugar
½ teaspoon	salt
2 tablespoons	unsalted butter
2	eggs
½ cup	water

GLAZE

6 tablespoons	unsalted butter
½ cup	brown sugar
1 teaspoon	ground cinnamon

1. Add all of the ingredients for the dough in the order suggested by your bread machine manual and process on the dough cycle according to the manufacturer's directions.

2. When the dough cycle ends, remove the dough from the machine. Preheat the oven to 350 degrees.

3. Grease a 10-inch tube pan heavily with 2 tablespoons of butter from the glaze ingredients. Sprinkle the pan with 2 tablespoons of brown sugar. Mix the remaining brown sugar with the cinnamon.

4. Melt the remaining 4 tablespoons butter. Divide the dough into 12 pieces. Roll each piece into a ball. Roll each ball in melted butter, then in the brown sugar-cinnamon mixture. Place the balls of dough in the tube pan 1 inch apart. When the first layer is completed, make a second layer, arranging the remaining balls of dough in an alternate position to those below so that they rest over the spaces. As they rise, the balls will expand. Cover with a clean kitchen towel and let rise for 30 minutes, or until doubled in size.

5. Bake 25 to 30 minutes. Turn out of pan immediately. Eat warm or let cool. Either pull apart or slice.

Savory Spirals

This is one of the easiest, least time-consuming ways to make party food ahead, or to fill up your freezer so that you are always ready for unexpected guests.

Yield: about 72 pieces

DOUGH

---

1 teaspoon	active dry yeast
2¼ cups	bread flour
¼ cup	cracked wheat
1 tablespoon	sugar
1 teaspoon	salt
1 tablespoon	vegetable oil
¾ cup plus 2 tablespoons	water

FILLINGS

Salami and mustard
Smoked salmon or smoked trout
Crumbled blue cheese and/or crumbled cooked bacon
Liver pâté
Chopped anchovies and chopped fresh parsley
Sliced green or black olives
Butter and chopped fresh herbs (parsley, cilantro, basil, dill, chives, or thyme)

1. Add all ingredients for the dough in the order suggested by your bread machine manual and process on the dough cycle according to the manufacturer's directions.

2. At the end of the dough cycle, remove the dough from the machine. Preheat the oven to 350 degrees. Grease two 9-by-5-by-3-inch loaf pans.

3. Divide the dough into 4 equal pieces. On a floured surface with a floured rolling pin, roll out each piece into a 4-by-8-inch rectangle. Spread each rectangle with a thin coat of the same or different fillings. Roll up jelly-roll fashion from a long end of each. Place 2 rolls side-by-side, seam side-down, in each loaf pan. Let rise 30 minutes, or until doubled in size.

4. Bake 30 minutes. Separate spirals while still warm. Let cool, then cut into ½-inch slices for hors d'oeuvre spirals.

New Orleans French Market Beignets

For a leisurely brunch, serve these hot out of the pan while guests sip café au lait *and nibble on fruit and cheese. Or prepare the dough a few hours ahead and refrigerate it. Cook the beignets after you come in from skating or hiking, and serve with hot chocolate or cider.*

Yield: 30 beignets

DOUGH

¾ cup	milk
1½ teaspoons	active dry yeast
1¾ cups	bread flour
2 tablespoons	sugar
½ teaspoon	grated nutmeg
½ teaspoon	salt
1	egg
2 to 4 cups	vegetable oil

COATINGS

¼ cup	confectioners' sugar
	or
¼ cup	granulated sugar
1 teaspoon	ground cinnamon

1. Add all ingredients for the dough except the oil in the order suggested by your bread machine manual and process on the dough cycle according to the manufacturer's directions.

2. When the dough cycle ends, remove the dough from the machine. On a floured surface with a floured rolling pin, roll out the dough into a rectangle about 10 by 12 inches. Cut into 2-by-2-inch squares to form the beignets. Place on greased trays, cover, and let rise 30 minutes, or until doubled in size.

3. In a wok or large saucepan, heat the oil to 365 degrees for deep frying. Fry 3 or 4 beignets at a time for 10 to 15 seconds on one side until golden, turn carefully, and fry the other side until lightly browned. Drain quickly on crumpled brown paper bags or on several layers of newspaper covered with a sheet of paper towel.

4. To coat the beignets, shake a few at a time in a paper bag with either confectioners' sugar or a blend of the granulated sugar and cinnamon.

DOUGHNUTS: In step 2, cut with a 3-inch doughnut cutter instead of a knife. The cooking time will be the same.

Marbled Brown and White Bread

This is great party bread to serve along with a platter of cold meats and cheeses. When you slice the bread it will have a handsome black and white swirl through each slice.

Yield: 2 loaves

2 teaspoons	active dry yeast
2 cups	bread flour
1 cup	whole wheat flour
1½ tablespoons	sugar
1½ teaspoons	salt
1½ tablespoons	vegetable oil
¾ cup	sourdough starter (page 7) *
1 cup	water
1 teaspoon	caramel coloring**

1. Add all ingredients except the caramel coloring in the order suggested by your bread machine manual and process on the dough cycle according to the manufacturer's directions. At the end of the dough cycle, remove the dough from the machine. Preheat the oven to 350 degrees.

2. Divide the dough in half. Cover one half; return the other half to the machine. Add the caramel coloring and process on the dough cycle again.

3. When the beeper sounds (or at the end of the first kneading in the Panasonic or National), remove the dark dough and divide in half. Roll half of the dark dough into an 8-by-12-inch rectangle. Roll half of the reserved light dough into an 8-by-12-inch rectangle. Put the light dough on top of the dark dough and roll up from a long side jelly-roll fashion. Repeat with the other halves to make 2 loaves.

4. Place the 2 loaves in greased 9-by-5-by-3-inch metal loaf pans. Let rise 30 minutes, or until doubled in size. Bake 30 minutes, until loaves sound hollow when bottoms are tapped.

* After measuring out what is needed for this recipe, be sure to replenish your sourdough starter with equal amounts of flour and water.

** Mail-order source on page 11.

Greek Easter Bread

Here is an elegantly simple centerpiece for the Easter table, sweet and perfumed with anise and orange. Serve as part of Easter breakfast or to end the dinner. Be sure to color eggs in advance with Easter egg coloring, not food coloring, so that the colors will not run. And make sure they are completely dry. Pink and lavender eggs look especially pretty.

Yield: 1 large bread, serving 8

2 teaspoons	active dry yeast
3 cups	bread flour
½ cup	sugar
1 teaspoon	salt
1 tablespoon	grated orange zest
1 teaspoon	anise or fennel seeds
4 tablespoons	unsalted butter
½ cup	water
3	eggs, beaten
3	colored hard-boiled eggs (Easter eggs)

1. Add all ingredients except 1 tablespoon of beaten egg and the colored eggs to the bread machine in the order suggested by your bread machine manual and process on the dough cycle according to the manufacturer's directions.

2. At the end of the dough cycle, remove the dough from the machine. Preheat the oven to 350 degrees. Divide the dough into 3 equal pieces. Roll each piece into a rope at least 24 inches long. Braid the pieces together and bring the ends firmly together to form a wreath; pinch the ends to seal. Place on a greased cookie sheet. In the center of the wreath, place a greased ovenproof bowl to keep the middle open.

3. Place each colored egg into the bread by lifting a strand of the braid and pushing the egg firmly under it so that the egg is strapped into the wreath by the dough. Space the eggs at equal distances. Brush the wreath carefully with the reserved 1 tablespoon beaten egg, trying not to get any on the colored eggs as it will spot them. Let the dough rise until doubled in size, about 30 minutes.

4. Bake 15 minutes. Remove the bowl and bake 15 minutes longer, or until the wreath is golden brown.

Brie in Brioche

With cheese or meat in brioche only a basket of crudités and drinks are needed to make a party. This is best served at room temperature. If it is served too warm, the cheese will ooze out of the bread when it is sliced. If made a day ahead, refrigerate until four hours before serving.

Yield: a 1-kilo Brie in brioche or a 2-pound pâté or meat loaf in brioche, serving 20 for cocktails.

DOUGH

1½ teaspoons	active dry yeast
2 cups	bread flour
1 tablespoon	sugar
1 teaspoon	salt
4 tablespoons (½ stick)	unsalted butter
2	eggs
½ cup	water

FILLING

---

1 kilo (2.2 pounds)	Brie
	or
2 pounds	country pâté
	or
	cooked meat loaf

---

1   egg, beaten

1. Add all ingredients for the dough in the order suggested by your bread machine manual and process on the dough cycle according to the manufacturer's directions.

2. At the end of the dough cycle, remove the dough from the machine. Preheat the oven to 375 degrees.

3. On a floured surface with a floured rolling pin, roll the dough into a circle at least 16 inches in diameter. Cut off a 1-inch-wide strip from one side and reserve. Place the circle minus the edge on a greased cookie sheet. Place the Brie in the center. Wrap the cheese in the dough, pleating or folding as you overlap the edges to make an attractive, sealed package. The cheese should be completely enclosed. Roll the reserved piece of dough into a rope. Tie a knot in the middle. Place the knot in the center of the wrapped cheese and tuck the ends under so the package looks tied. Brush with the beaten egg glaze.

4. Let the dough rise 30 minutes. Bake 25 minutes, or until golden brown all over.

PÂTÉ OR MEAT LOAF IN BRIOCHE: Substitute 2 pounds of your favorite country pâté or cooked meat loaf. The baking time will be the same.

Bagels

In my family there are two kinds of bagels: hot, fresh bagels to eat and cold bagels for doorstops. Now you, too, can have the eating kind. Slice them and smear with butter or cream cheese. Add a sprinkling of scallions and thin slices of smoked salmon, if you like. Top a bagel half with a slice of tomato and cheese and broil to make instant individual pizza.

Yield: 8 bagels

DOUGH

1½ teaspoons	active dry yeast
2 cups	bread flour
1½ tablespoons	sugar
1 teaspoon	salt
¾ cup	water
1 tablespoon	barley malt syrup *

TOPPINGS

2 tablespoons	poppy seeds, sesame seeds, kosher salt, or minced ' onion

1. Add all ingredients for the dough except the barley malt syrup in the order suggested by your bread machine manual and process on the dough cycle according to the manufacturer's directions.

2. At the end of the dough cycle, remove the dough from the machine. Preheat the oven to 375 degrees. In a large pot bring 2 quarts of water to a boil.

3. While the water comes to a boil, divide the dough into 8 pieces. Roll each piece into a rope 12 inches long. Make a circle of each piece, overlapping the ends by at least an inch and pressing or rolling the overlap tightly to seal. Let the bagels rise for only 5 minutes.

4. Add the malt syrup to the boiling water. (The syrup gives the bagels their golden crust.) Lower a few bagels at a time into the boiling water. As soon as the bagels rise to the top, remove with a skimmer or spatula to a lightly greased baking sheet. Sprinkle about ¾ teaspoon of any of the toppings over each bagel and bake 20 minutes, or until golden.

* Available in health food stores.

Holiday Morning Sticky Buns

Whether these are called honey buns, cinnamon buns, or sticky buns, they are sweet and delicious. I like to save them for a holiday breakfast because they are such a special buttery, gooey treat.

Yield: 18 large buns

DOUGH

1¼ teaspoons	active dry yeast
2 cups	bread flour
2 tablespoons	sugar
2 tablespoons	unsalted butter
½ teaspoon	salt
2	eggs
½ cup	water

TOPPING AND FILLING

4 tablespoons	unsalted butter, softened
¾ cup	brown sugar
1 cup	pecans, chopped (optional)
¼ cup	honey
½ teaspoon	ground cinnamon
½ cup	currants or raisins

1. Add all ingredients for the dough in the order suggested by your bread manual and process on the basic dough cycle according to the manufacturer's directions.

2. At the end of the dough cycle, remove the dough from the machine. Preheat the oven to 350 degrees. Grease two 9-by-11-inch baking dishes heavily with the softened butter for the topping. Sprinkle 2 tablespoons of the brown sugar and half the pecans over the butter in each pan. Drizzle on the honey.

3. On a floured surface with a floured rolling pin, roll out the dough into a 9-by-18-inch rectangle. Sprinkle ¼ cup of the brown sugar, the cinnamon, and the raisins over the dough. Roll up jelly-roll fashion from one of the long sides. Cut the dough into eighteen 1-inch slices. (You can freeze some of the buns at this point.)

4. Place the buns, cut side-down, in the prepared baking dishes. Let rise 20 minutes. Bake 20 minutes, and immediately invert baking pan onto a serving platter.

Challah

This is the Jewish Sabbath egg bread, the sacramental bread blessed along with the wine. Tender, slightly sweet, and a lovely golden color, it makes wonderful eating all on its own or with butter and jam. Day-old challah thickly sliced makes first-rate French toast. If you don't care about the traditional braided shape, you can throw all the ingredients into your bread machine and process completely on the basic bread cycle and omit the glaze.

SMALL LOAF (1 POUND)	INGREDIENTS	LARGE LOAF (1½ POUNDS)
DOUGH		
1½ teaspoons	active dry yeast	2¼ teaspoons
¾ cup plus 2 tablespoons	bread flour	2¾ cups plus 1 tablespoon
¼ cup	sugar	¼ cup plus 2 tablespoons
½ teaspoon	salt	¾ teaspoon
2 tablespoons plus 1 teaspoon	vegetable oil	3½ tablespoons
2	egg yolks	3
⅔ cup	water	1 cup
GLAZE		
1 egg, beaten		

1. Add all ingredients for the dough in the order suggested by your bread machine manual and process on the dough cycle according to the manufacturer's directions.

2. At the end of the dough cycle, remove the dough from the machine and divide it into 3 equal pieces. Form each piece into a round, pressing to break any air bubbles. Place on a lightly greased plate or cookie sheet, leaving room for the balls of dough to double in size. Cover with a clean bowl or kitchen towel and let rise about 20 minutes in a warm—but not hot—draft-free place. If you press the dough lightly with your finger and the mark remains, the dough is ready. If the indentation springs out again, the dough needs to rise longer.

3. Preheat the oven to 350 degrees. Roll each piece of dough into a rope about 18 inches long. Braid the ropes together, pinching the dough together at both ends to seal and tucking the ends under.

4. Place the braid on a baking sheet. Brush the egg glaze over the loaf. Let rise again for 30 minutes, or until doubled in size. Bake the challah 30 minutes, or until the bottom is golden brown and the bread sounds hollow when tapped on the bottom. Let the loaf cool before slicing.

Bibliography

Amendola, Joseph. *The Bakers' Manual*. Rochelle Park. New Jersey: Hayden Books, 1972.

Beck, Simone: Bertholle, Louisette; Child, Julia. *Mastering the Art of French Cooking*. New York: Alfred A. Knopf, 1961.

Clayton, Bernard, Jr. *The Breads of France*. New York: Bobbs-Merrill, 1978.

Cutler, Kathy. *The Festive Bread Book*. Woodbury, New York: Barrons, 1982.

Field, Carol. *The Italian Baker*. New York: Harper and Row, 1985.

German, Donna Rathmell. *The Bread Machine Cookbook*. San Leandro, California: Bristol Publishing, 1991.

Honig, Mariana. *Breads of the World*. New York: Chelsea House, 1977.

Jones, Judith and Evan. *The Book of Bread*. New York: Harper and Row, 1982.

Katzen, Mollie. *The Enchanted Broccoli Forest*. Berkeley, California: Ten Speed Press, 1982.

Lukins, Sheila and Rosso, Julee. *Silver Palate Good Times Cookbook*. New York: Workman, 1984.

Ojakangas, Beatrice. *Great Wholegrain Breads*. New York: E. P. Dutton, 1984.

Tarr, Yvonne Young. *The New York Times Bread and Soup Cookbook*. New York: Ballantine Books, 1972.

Index